Sorry we couldn'[t get]
the real thing!

Enjoy!

Happy Birthday Jim

Love

Anne, Eric & Oscar

x x x

May 2010

Honda
Gold Wing

Haynes

Great Bikes

Honda
Gold Wing

Ian Falloon

First published in 2001
Reprinted 2003

A catalogue record for this book is available from the British Library

ISBN 1 85960 660 1

Library of Congress catalog card no. 2001132577

Published by Haynes Publishing, Sparkford,
Yeovil, Somerset BA22 7JJ, UK

Tel. 01963 442030 Fax 01963 440001
Int. tel. +44 1963 442030 Fax +44 1963 440001
E-mail: sales@haynes-manuals.co.uk
Web site: www.haynes.co.uk

Haynes North America, Inc.,
861 Lawrence Drive, Newbury Park,
California 91320, USA

Printed and bound in England by J. H. Haynes & Co. Ltd, Sparkford

Contents

Introduction and acknowledgements

Although it started life as a touring motorcycle, the Gold Wing has transcended this to become a phenomenon. Gold Wing owners are unlike other motorcyclists, and owning one of these machines ensures entry into a unique world. Here, pride of ownership and camaraderie are the essence, and with one of the most loyal customer followings, the Gold Wing is endorsed by nine out of ten owners who claim they would buy another. Despite imitations the Gold Wing represents the pinnacle of motorcycle touring and remains unique, more than 25 years after it first appeared. The Gold Wing was also the first Japanese motorcycle designed purely with the American market in mind. Soon, it was so successful that it became an American motorcycle and it is now only produced in the United States, at the Honda Motorcycle Plant in Marysville, Ohio. When Honda designed the Gold Wing they managed a marketing triumph. This was their first motorcycle with 'America' written all over it. It had everything: size, luxury, comfort, reliability, and gadgetry. In America, size and weight matter. Bigger is better and luxury is determined by the number of gadgets. The Gold Wing became to represent the definition of the American motorcycle through its size, spaciousness, weight and sophistication. From that first Gold Wing of 1975 emerged a complete touring experience. Here was a mandate for the open road, with no pretence at universitality, and one that has grown as the demands of the market has required.

What sets the Gold Wing apart from most other motorcycles is the endurance of the design. Take a ten-year-old catalogue of production motorcycles today, and only a handful of models will be found to have survived. Look at a 25-year-old catalogue and the Gold Wing stands out as a name and concept that has endured, and has stood the test of time. The big Honda immediately set the standard for touring performance in terms of ride, reliability, and comfort. The engine was strong enough to haul the largest load, and the design perfect for its intended purpose. The Gold Wing was, and continues to represent, the acme of touring performance and now, as it continues to grow in capacity and provide an even wider range of comfort and luxury features, it is set to attract a larger group of riders.

The Gold Wing is much more than a superb touring motorcycle. Although initially slow to catch on, it soon garnered a cult following. Exceeding normal parameters it opened the door to a new group of owners and riders. Middle America wholeheartedly embraced the Gold Wing and it has become almost a two-wheeled Winnebago. They are generally superbly presented but their owners spend more time riding than polishing them. Singularity of purpose is always the first step towards cultism and there is no more unique touring bike than the Gold Wing. Clubs sprouted up all over America, and soon worldwide. A Gold Wing ensured camaraderie and involvement in a growing cult. With an expanding aftermarket industry for accessories the Gold Wing also became the perfect vehicle for an owner to display individuality. Yet unlike some other single-model followings, a Gold Wing isn't elitist. They may be expensive but they aren't rare and a Gold Wing in many ways represents the true essence of motorcycling. Friendship, activities, individuality, and the joy of being on the road.

Here, I have endeavoured to chronicle the history of the Gold Wing and Valkyrie since 1975, emphasising the technical development and covering all official incarnations through until the new GL 1800 for 2001. I have also tried to provide an insight into the Gold Wing character. Owning a Gold Wing is about individuality, and most sport an aftermarket accessory of some kind. As the Gold Wing aftermarket is huge, and big business, many customised bikes have been featured. Roy Kidney kindly provided magnificent photographs of modified Gold Wings in California, and the magazine archives of *Cycle* and *Cycle World* also proved especially rewarding. My thanks must go to *Cycle World* editor David Edwards, and executive editor Brian Catterson. Again Ken Wootton, editor of *Australian Motorcycle News*, and Jeremy Bowdler, editor of *Two Wheels*, allowed access to their photographic archives. Pete ter Horst, motorcycle press manager for American Honda Motor Co. Inc., provided information on the 2001 Gold Wing, and Darwin Holmstrom and Jeff Hackett filled in some important historical gaps in photographic material. Throughout this project I received continual support from Darryl Reach, former Editorial Director of Haynes's Special Interest Publishing Division. Again, none of this would have been possible without the support of my wife Miriam, and sons Benjamin and Timothy.

The king of motorcycles

Now enjoying unparalleled success as the definitive touring motorcycle, and entrenched as a mainstream motorcycle, this wasn't always the case for the Honda Gold Wing. Back in 1972 the idea of a large-capacity, liquid-cooled flat-four shaft-drive motorcycle was quite radical. In terms of ultimate all-round performance the air-cooled four-cylinder across-the-frame four-cylinder motorcycle with chain final drive ruled. Honda itself had set the standard with their four-cylinder CB 750 of 1968, but this had been overtaken by the 903cc Kawasaki Z1 in 1972. But not all companies were committed to the now-ubiquitous four, and this was a period where new designs were continually being released to tempt an expanding market. The year 1968 saw Kawasaki's astounding 500cc two-stroke three-cylinder H1, followed by an even faster and wilder 750cc H2. Suzuki followed with their GT750, a three-cylinder liquid-cooled 750cc two-stroke, and Yamaha decided a 750cc TX750 parallel twin four-stroke was the way to go. On a smaller scale the European factories also decided to expand their line-ups into larger capacity machines. Moto Guzzi released their V7, a 90° V-twin with shaft final drive; Triumph and Laverda produced three-cylinder four-strokes, and Ducati took a different direction with their 90° V-twin. So diverse were all these designs that they were almost

The six-cylinder M1 was the Gold Wing's forerunner. This featured a BMW-like rear section and was later used as a model for the GL 1500. (American Honda)

corporate statements of an individual factory's capability to produce a high-performance motorcycle. Additionally, some companies resisted the temptation for experimentation, notably Harley-Davidson and BMW. While BMW revamped their boxer twin with the R75/5, these two marques maintained a commitment to evolution rather than revolution, and they in turn would heavily influence the Gold Wing.

It was within this climate of diversity that Soichiro Honda, the founder of the Honda company, expressed the desire for a new flagship; the largest, fastest, and best grand touring machine ever produced. He wanted to create the 'King of Motorcycles', so in the autumn of 1972, a group of engineers met in one of the many committee rooms at the Honda factory in Wako, in Southern Japan to discuss this project. At that meeting there were many of those responsible for some of Honda's most successful designs of the 1960s, including the brilliant Soichiro Irimajiri. Irimajiri headed the design for the amazing five and six-cylinder road racing engines during the 1960s and would later give Honda the highly successful CX500 V-twin, and the astonishing six-cylinder CBX 1000. Eventually he became Honda Motorcycle R&D Vice-President and was responsible for the oval piston NR500 Grand Prix machine of 1979. Later he would move to be head of American Honda. However, his brief for now would be to head the team to design the 'King of Motorcycles'. What was needed, Irimajiri told his colleagues, was a machine to uphold Honda's corporate pride in the face of the new opposition. They needed a machine that would be acclaimed as the world's fastest, and best, grand tourer.

Drawing heavily on existing designs the machine these designers produced was unlike any other seen before. Code-named the M1 (but also known as the AOK), only one example was made, but it set the scene for the later Gold Wing. The heart of the M1 was a 1,470cc six-cylinder engine, the cylinders arranged in a horizontally opposed layout similar to the BMW. Unlike the BMW though, the engine was liquid-cooled, and there was a single overhead camshaft on each bank of cylinders. The bore and stroke were 72 x 60mm, and the compression ratio a very mild 8.0:1. Breathing through a downdraft two-barrel carburettor the power was 80hp at 6,700rpm. That may not sound like much for a nearly 1500cc engine by modern standards, but it was about on a par with the 900cc Kawasaki Z1, and the M1 was meant as a touring motorcycle.

Housing this almost automotive-like engine was a double cradle frame with engine mountings similar to a CB750. The entire rear of the motorcycle seemed to come straight off a BMW, including the gearbox, driveshaft, rear hub, seat, and mufflers. Considering the size of the engine the M1 weighed in at a surprisingly low 220kg (484lb), and had a very moderate wheelbase of 1,480mm (58.25in). The tyres were normal for the period: a 3.25 x 19-inch on the front and 4.00 x 18-inch on the rear, and there was a 20-litre fuel tank. Not surprisingly, given the power of the engine, the M1 also performed reasonably strongly for such a large machine. The top speed was said to be in the region of 130mph (210kph), with a standing start quarter-mile time of around 12 seconds. As to be expected of a flat six, the engine smoothness was reported to be exceptional, and the handling very stable due to the low centre of gravity. It may have looked rather ungainly and odd with the roughly finished engine and BMW rear end, but the main problem with the M1 was the length of the engine. This made a respectable riding position difficult to achieve and the M1 was relegated to the scrap heap. The design fundamentals weren't forgotten though, and when the 'King

Soichiro Honda

Born in 1906, the eldest son of a poor blacksmith, Soichiro Honda became fascinated with machines as a child, particularly cars. After only eight years of education he then went out to find his fortune, and by the 1930s was already a successful racing car driver and builder. A near-fatal crash changed his direction, and in 1937 he set up a company, Tokai Seiki Heavy Industries, to manufacture piston rings. In order to produce a superior product Honda went back to school to study metallurgy, study that would later yield benefits when he engaged in motorcycle production. During the Second World War his plant produced aircraft propellers but bombing and an earthquake destroyed his factories and he sold the company to Toyota. He then embarked on a series of entrepreneurial schemes, including homemade whisky, until he founded Honda Technical Laboratory in 1948 and began to adapt war-surplus two-stroke engines to bicycles. Such was the demand for cheap transportation that this enterprise grew and when the supply of war-surplus engines ran out Honda joined investor Takeo Fujisawa to form the Honda Motor Company in September 1948. Soichiro Honda's intention was always to produce complete motorcycles and in 1949 Honda became the first post-war Japanese manufacturer to produce both an engine and frame. The resulting single-cylinder two-stroke D-type Dream was a runaway success, much of this being due to the marketing ability of his co-director Takeo Fujisawa. From then on there was nothing to stop the expansion of Honda in Japan, but Soichiro Honda had other visions for his company. In June 1954, he went to the Isle of Man for the TT races for the first time, returning to Japan dismayed at the power and performance of the finest European racing motorcycles.

Undeterred, Honda remained determined and ambitious. By 1957, the first exports had begun, and in 1959 he returned to the Isle of Man, this time with a batch of 125cc racers. Although outpaced, Honda took the 125cc manufacturers' team trophy. It was a harbinger of the future. Within five years they would dominate world championship racing and by 1967 had amassed 16 world championships and 137 grand prix victories. Throughout this period the company grew dramatically and exports grew from under 50,000 machines in 1961 to over 338,000 only two years later. That year American sales alone topped 100,000.

Soichiro Honda had always had a vision for his company, and that was to create the greatest motorcycle empire in the world. In the pursuit of this not only did Honda engage in competition at all levels, but they also invested heavily in automated manufacturing equipment, advertising and promotion. Honda was very much a hands-on company director. He would often be seen among the workers in the manufacturing and research departments working on technical solutions and sorting out problems. In 1973, both Soichiro Honda and Takeo Fujisawa stepped down, but Honda retained the title of Supreme Adviser and was determined to see one final project through; that of a true flagship to showcase Honda technology – the 'King of Motorcycles'. Soichiro not only saw this vision come to fruition, but witnessed the Gold Wing going on to become one of the most successful of all Honda motorcycles. When he died on 5 August 1991, the Gold Wing remained unsurpassed as the ultimate touring motorcycle and a true testimony to his extraordinary vision.

Soichiro Honda, the man responsible for the largest and most successful motorcycle company in the world, and the Gold Wing. (Honda UK)

of Motorcycles' project continued it was heavily influenced by the M1. Later too, the six-cylinder M1 engine would be bolted into a GL 1200 chassis to test the feasibility of the GL 1500.

After discarding the M1, Honda decided a flat-four was a more practical solution than the flat-six, and set up a new design team to head the project, now titled Project 371. Toshio Nozue took over from Irimajiri as project leader and set about creating an innovative world-beating grand tourer. Like Irimajiri, Nozue also came to Project 371 with impressive credentials, although he was essentially a frame designer. Already to his credit was the CB 750 and two-stroke 250cc Elsinore off-road machine. The 'King of Motorcycles' was also now to be known as the 'Gold Wing', after the company emblem.

The engine needed to be larger than the Kawasaki Z1, BMW R90S, and the Moto Guzzi V7, and more powerful than the Harley-Davidson FLH-1200. Thus the eventual size was 999cc, with an oversquare bore and stroke of 72 x 61.4mm. Many of the features were inherited from the prototype M1, and the flat-four layout necessitated liquid-cooling. Also, as with the M1, there was a single overhead camshaft on each cylinder bank, these being driven by toothed rubber belts on the new engine. Although relatively new to motorcycles at that time (only the Moto Morini 3½ was featuring them), they were already widely used in automotive applications. Honda was by that time a successful car manufacturer, and these timing belts were identical to those on the Honda Civic.

The Honda team believed they had the first liquid-cooled motorcycle, but their knowledge of motorcycle history was flawed and they overlooked the remarkable two-stroke Scott, a British motorcycle that had featured liquid-cooling as far back as 1908. Another feature

that was unusual for a motorcycle, but also not pioneering, was the location of the fuel tank under the seat. The Gold Wing 'tank' thus contained a glove box, tool kit, radiator coolant tank, a myriad of electrical components, and an emergency kickstart lever.

With four motorcycle-type 32mm Keihin constant vacuum carburettors, the power from the first 999cc Gold Wing engine was a moderate 80hp at 7,500rpm. Drive to the five-speed gearbox was via a motorcycle-type multi-plate clutch rather than a BMW automotive-style single plate, and the final drive was by shaft. The biggest advancement for a motorcycle with an in-line crankshaft was the use of the ac generator as a counter rotating flywheel to cancel out the torque reaction of the crankshaft. For many prospective buyers of touring machines this feature alone had kept them away from the BMW with its reported severe torque reaction, and opened the Gold Wing to a whole new world of touring motorcyclists.

As Honda's first production motorcycle with a shaft final drive, this took longer to develop than other components. In those days before CAD stress analysis, testing included brutally abusing the drivetrain by shifting into first gear while rolling at 50kph (30mph) in neutral. This abnormal torture gave violent rear wheel hopping, but provided engineers with information on the strength of the driveshaft.

Completing the specification were triple disc brakes, and a fat (for the day) 4.50H 17A Bridgestone Superspeed 21-R2 rear tyre specially developed for the 265kg (584lb) dry Gold Wing. There was also a suggestion in the press during 1975 that Honda spent £500,000 just developing the rear tyre alone, although Toshio Nozue denied this. The tyre size was inspired by that of the Harley-

The first production GL 1000 of 1975 was remarkably similar to the final prototype. (American Honda)

Davidson Electra Glide, but unlike the Harley the Gold Wing came with a more conventional 19-inch front wheel, this having a 3.50H 19 Bridgestone Superspeed 21-F2 tyre. The wheels were wire spoked, a quality touch being the aluminium wheel rims, and the overall physical size was cleverly kept to a minimum. Even the wheelbase was a fairly moderate 1,540mm (60.6in). As Honda considered the Gold Wing very important, the prototype underwent longer testing than the usual eight months, with development riders punishing the machine for a year at the Tochigi test facility. The testers found the low centre-of-gravity provided excellent stability and resistance to side winds, although they found the machine very difficult to pick up if it fell over. The final version was conservatively styled, with simple logos and minimal pinstriping, and so good was the final prototype that only three small features were changed for the first GL 1000 KO production

The competition: Harley-Davidson and BMW

The primary market for the 'King of Motorcycles' was always America. If you wanted a large capacity touring machine in the United States in the early 1970s there really was no alternative to Harley-Davidson's FLH-1200 Electra Glide. Despite an ancient 87 x 100mm 1,207cc air-cooled overhead valve V-twin, and a clunky four-speed gearbox, the Electra Glide offered then unparalleled cross-country performance. Luxury, prestige, comfort, and reliability were all words used to describe the Electra Glide experience. Although the engine had changed little for decades, by 1974 standard features included footboards, windshield, white-wall tyres, saddlebags, warning flashers, lots of chrome, dual front disc brakes, and a security alarm system. With the plushest seat in motorcycling, and huge tyres giving reasonable wear and cornering, the gigantic 328kg (722lb) Electra Glide enjoyed a huge following. It may not have been very refined, but the Electra Glide set the touring standard for a motorcycle in the United States.

The other main source of competition in the touring market emanated from Europe, in the form of the flat-twin BMW. In 1969, the BMW had grown to 750cc, with the R75/5, and was enlarged further in 1973, to 900cc with the 90/6. In many ways, BMW pursued a similar policy of continual development to Harley-Davidson, and they had been evolving their air-cooled flat-twin engine since 1923. This layout readily lent itself to a shaft final drive but the in-line crankshaft also gave an unpleasant torque reaction, particularly during heavy acceleration or when tweaking the throttle with the bike at rest. The BMW was also a more European-style sports tourer, with an emphasis on all-round capability rather than only being applicable to the straight US Interstate highways. Thus, compared with the Harley-Davidson, the BMW was light and agile, and when

As the Gold Wing was always intended for America, much of the impetus for its design came from the Harley-Davidson Electra Glide. Although unrefined, this epitomised American motorcycle touring. (Jeff Hackett)

developed into the R90/S considerably more sporting. An R90/S weighed only 205kg (451lb) and with 67hp on tap, provided acceptable, if certainly not blinding, acceleration, and a 200kph (124mph) top speed. Where the BMW really suffered in the USA was in its gross vehicle weight limit. Americans like to load up their vehicles and the maximum of the R90/6 and R90/S was easily exceeded. Because the BMW was also produced in lower numbers than a Japanese motorcycle, and for a different customer, it wasn't really considered a true competitor to Honda's new touring machine. However, many of the design features were considered essential by the Honda design team, and the BMW was a strong influence on the eventual 'King of Motorcycles.' In many ways the Gold Wing was a synthesis of the best touring features of both the Harley-Davidson Electra Glide and BMW. Honda wanted to create a new market, and saw the Harley as being for hippies and Hell's Angels while the BMW was a more short-distance touring machine. In the Gold Wing Honda believed it had the first true long-distance touring motorcycle.

The European idea of a touring motorcycle was considerably more sporting than that of the Harley-Davidson. The most sporting BMW of the mid-1970s was the R90S. (Ian Falloon)

version. The self-cancelling turn indicators were removed and there was a different radiator cap which now included a warning sticker.

Although there were rumours circulating for some time prior to its release as to the size and layout of the Gold Wing, Honda successfully kept the actual configuration secret. Hearsay indicated a larger, conventional CB 750-style engine, or even a V-six. The speculation was laid to rest when the first Gold Wing, the GL 1000 K0, was released at the Cologne Show in October 1974. After concentrating on building their automotive division, work on the CVCC engine in particular occupying resources for some time, the Gold Wing was also the first significant new Honda motorcycle since the CB 750.

Technical appraisal

Although the Gold Wing seemed revolutionary in 1975, the reality was that none of the seemingly innovative features was especially new. What Toshio Nozue and his team had successfully done was take several unusual characteristics, both automotive and motorcycle, and successfully combine them together in a single design for the first time. We have already seen that liquid-cooling had featured on the Scott motorcycle, and toothed

rubber camshaft drive belts on the slightly earlier Moto Morini 3½. Both BMW and Moto Guzzi already had shaft final drive. However, the entire Gold Wing concept was so different that these features, and others, seemed almost revolutionary for a mainstream motorcycle at the time. What really set the Gold Wing apart was its overall size, combined with an engine that provided Superbike performance with automotive-like service intervals and reliability.

The engine and drivetrain

The new engine really was the heart of the Gold Wing, and apart from the rather obscure two-stroke Silk, itself a development of the Scott, there was no other liquid-cooled street motorcycle available in 1973. So when the Gold Wing project began Honda engineers studied the best existing automotive designs. They wanted the engine to be as compact and smooth as possible so they looked at the Porsche, BMW and Chevrolet designs. Like a Porsche flat-six engine, the crankcases were split vertically at the centre, but the Gold Wing featured a unique crankshaft locating system. With one half of the crankshaft main bearings in unit with the right-side crankcase, caps then held the crankshaft to the right crankcase with three 40mm main bearings, one at each end and one in the centre. The crankpins were set at 180° to each other, sitting in between each bearing journal and the con-rod journals were 43mm in diameter. In

effect, the engine was two 180° parallel twins set beside the other, with the right-side cylinders staggered forward. The cylinders were in one piece with the crankcase halves and when the left crankcase was removed the pistons exited from the bottom of the cylinders. Removal of the right cylinders required the unbolting of the con-rods and the pistons and the rods then came out through the top of the cylinders.

This casting of the cylinders with the crankcase halves was normal liquid-cooled automotive practice, also considerably reducing manufacturing costs. The only disadvantage was that piston or ring replacement was more difficult, and required engine removal from the frame. However, given the automotive nature of the Gold Wing engine design the service intervals promised were considerably longer than that of other motorcycle engines. The Gold Wing engine also seemed to be designed with the idea

Undoubtedly the distinctive 999cc flat-four engine with its four individual Keihin carburettors dominated the Gold Wing. This provided unrivalled smoothness, and Superbike performance. (Roy Kidney)

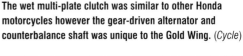

The three-main-bearing crankshaft was retained in the right-side crankcase half. Also evident is the Hy-Vo primary drive to the clutch and transmission and front toothed belt camshaft drive. (*Cycle*)

The wet multi-plate clutch was similar to other Honda motorcycles however the gear-driven alternator and counterbalance shaft was unique to the Gold Wing. (*Cycle*)

of a larger engine in mind as there were very thick cast-iron cylinder liners cast into the aluminium blocks, with very wide spacing between the cylinder centres.

All earlier air-cooled Honda engines had featured a gudgeon pin off-set by 1mm to the rear of the piston centreline to reduce piston noise generated by the extra piston-to-cylinder bore clearance. Now, with a thermostat controlling the coolant temperature, and thus the rate of expansion of the cylinder, tighter piston-to-bore clearances could be used. This made offset gudgeon pins unnecessary, but unlike most motorcycle engines there was no gudgeon retainer in the piston. The gudgeon was a press fit in the small end, and a press needed to be used to centre the gudgeon during assembly. With the piston being a loose fit on the gudgeon lubrication on the right side came from oil flung from the crankshaft. The left cylinders required holes in the rods to supply more oil. Because identical con-rods were used on both sides the right-side rods featured a plain bearing without a feed hole to block the oil supply.

While the crankshaft with its three plain main bearings was undeniably automotive inspired, immediately behind the rear main bearing motorcycle technology made itself apparent. The primary drive was by a 25mm Hy-Vo chain (with a 24/41 reduction), similar to that on other Honda motorcycles of that time, like the CB 500 four.

This chain drove the outer clutch hub through a countershaft, with the inner clutch drum driving the gearbox mainshaft back through the countershaft. The mainshaft ran directly parallel and underneath the crankshaft, with a shock absorber incorporated in the centre of the countershaft Hy-Vo sprocket. To the right of the mainshaft was the layshaft, the rear gear driving another directly above it for the 25mm output shaft, this having a 40/33 reduction. Like most motorcycle designs, the engine and gearbox were constructed in a single unit, and as with most engines of the period, crankcase ventilation was by a breather tube into the atmosphere.

Further motorcycle features were apparent throughout the entire drivetrain, and the clutch and gearbox could almost have come from the CB 750. The wet multi-plate clutch comprised seven friction (from the CB 450 twin) and eight plain plates, but as only one of the two steel plates actually transmitted power, clutch failure was a problem on early models. The entire gearbox and selector mechanism was very similar to that of the CB 750. This even included identical ratios, although few parts were actually interchangeable. Continuing the family connection were the clutch springs, these being seen on the earlier CB 72 twin. Nozue was particularly proud of his engineering tour-de-force, the alternator and counterbalance shaft, this being driven by a straight-cut gear behind

Setting the Gold Wing engine apart from most motorcycle designs was the rubber-toothed belt drive to the pair of single overhead camshafts. Also driven from the front of the engine was the water pump. (*Cycle*)

the Hy-Vo primary drive. To overcome excessive noise, the matching counterbalance shaft gear was in two parts, each section being independently coupled to the shaft by splines with rubber inserts. As the counterbalance shaft was directly driven by gear rather than chain it rotated in the opposite direction to the crankshaft. There was an additional flywheel attached to the rear of the alternator, and to accentuate the cancellation of the torque reaction the speed of the countershaft was slightly higher than that of the crank. Unlike the CB 750 that featured a newer generation, excited-field alternator (this only produced the

power required), the Gold Wing reverted to a 300-watt fixed rate alternator that varied with engine speed to reduce any sudden effects in the anti-torque system. Excess power was then bled through an electronic valve.

If the lower end of the Gold Wing engine was a mixture of motorcycle and automotive practice, apart from the camshaft drive the top end was very much that of a motorcycle. The hemispherical cylinder heads had generously sized valves and ports indicating that the engine was in a moderately high state of tune. The inlet valves were 37mm, with 32mm exhaust valves, these being large for 250cc cylinders with a

These are the four Keihin carburettors bolted to a common airbox, allowing easier synchronisation and a single throttle control cable. (*Cycle*)

72mm bore. In order to fit these valves in the combustion chamber they were offset on opposite sides of the combustion chamber centreline, just like the CB 750. Also like the CB 750 was the valve and camshaft layout. The camshafts were in two sections and supported by aluminium bearings, these sharing the high pressure oil feed from the rockers. The camshaft timing too offered reasonably long duration for a touring motorcycle. The inlet valve opened at 5° before top dead centre, closing 50° after bottom dead centre, while the exhaust valve opened 50° before bottom dead centre and closed 5° after top dead centre. Both inlet and exhaust valve lift was 8.5mm. In a dry chamber in the front of the engine were the two 17mm 87-tooth rubber belts with trapezoidal teeth. A pair of spring-loaded pulleys tensioned these with service schedules calling for belt inspection every 24,000 miles (39,000km). The pistons provided a 9.2:1 compression ratio, and while the claimed power

was only 80bhp, this was undoubtedly pessimistic considering the performance. Perhaps Honda didn't want the Gold Wing to be embroiled in any horsepower contest with the Kawasaki Z1, given its touring orientation. Whatever the reason, the straight-line performance of the first Gold Wing placed it truly in the Superbike category.

The carburetion too was more motorcycle than car, with four individual Keihin 32mm constant vacuum carburettors. These carburettors breathed through a cast aluminium plenum chamber bolted to the top of the engine cases. They were also attached to a common air box, this easily being removed for carburettor synchronisation. There was a single-throttle cable, the chokes being joined by a fairly complex system of shaft connectors. This was also duplicated for the chokes. The fuel lines were incorporated in drilled passages in the airbox, and a fuel filter fitted between the fuel

The fuel tank that wasn't

The key slot at the rear of the 'tank' was the give away that this wasn't a tank at all, as lifting the flap upwards revealed. Where it was to be expected that there would be fuel, it was actually a small glove box with the usual poor-quality tool kit that typified motorcycles of that era. Lifting the plastic tray revealed the air cleaner and fuel filler cap, and after loosening a couple of retainers the sides of the 'tank' pivoted down. In the right side was the radiator coolant header tank, along with an emergency kickstart. This relic of an earlier motorcycle era could be easily fitted to a rig at the rear of the engine above the clutch and below the alternator, not that it would ever be required. Underneath the left cover were the electrical components, all systematically laid out and easily accessible. This looked to be a daunting display but there really weren't any more components than was average at the time. The glove box tray was also too small to be of any practical use, but the electric fuel gauge which was incorporated in the top panel was appreciated. It was also the first time such a feature had appeared on a motorcycle.

For the first time on a motorcycle there was an electric fuel gauge, although on early models like this 1976 Limited Edition it wasn't the most reliable. (Roy Kidney)

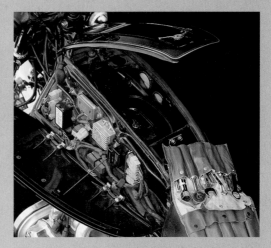

Lifting the panel in the top of the dummy fuel tank revealed a tray for the toolkit. On most Gold Wings this was of poor quality although the Limited Edition received a special kit in a leather pouch. The electrical components were housed under the left cover. (Roy Kidney)

tank valves and carburettors. Here was another clever deviation from usual motorcycle practice. The space normally occupying the fuel tank wasn't a fuel tank at all. In order to maintain a low centre of gravity the actual fuel tank was underneath the seat, between the frame tubes. However, the fuel level was now so close to that of the carburettor float level that an automotive-style fuel pump was needed to provide an adequate fuel supply. This was driven from the rear end of the right camshaft.

With the oil and water pump drive the Gold Wing engine did seem overly complex for a motorcycle. Here, a small duplex pump, chain-driven behind the clutch hub, connected with a long shaft running under the engine, parallel to the crankshaft. Thus there were three driving systems at the rear of the engine: the Hy-Vo primary, gear counterbalance, and the duplex oil and water pump. This slender longitudinal shaft drove three pumps, including a small clutch scavenge pump underneath the clutch hub. At the other end of the shaft was an Eaton-type trochoidal oil pump for the engine and gearbox, and the water pump impeller located on the left, front of the engine. The cooling system followed that of standard automotive practice, being thermostatically controlled with an electric fan activating in extreme circumstances. There was one more drive, that for the electric start, this being low on the left of the engine. Offering a combination of automotive and motorcycle features, the Gold Wing engine was unique, but also heavy. Without carburettors, but with oil, the engine weight was a considerable 96kg (212lb) which made the engine unit alone heavier than a complete 1975 CB 125 S2. No wonder the size and weight of the Gold Wing took some getting used to. Despite this considerable weight though, the engine was surprisingly compact. Almost cubic, with the carburettors attached it was 660mm wide, 533mm long, and 508mm high.

Weight aside, if there was anything that set the Gold Wing apart from other motorcycles in 1975 is was the absolute quietness of the engine. Undoubtedly the water jackets soaked up some of the noise, and the toothed belts were quieter than other camshaft drive systems. Yet most of the quietness came from the massive mufflers and the claimed noise level was only 77 decibels. The welded-together steel exhaust system was painted black, with a chrome shield and tailpipe. So efficient was this large and heavy system that it also tended to run cool and absorb water, often rusting out prematurely.

Another feature that made the Gold Wing appealing in its intended role as an unparalleled tourer was the shaft final drive. Previously the preserve of European marques such as BMW and Moto Guzzi, the incorporation of a driveshaft through the centre of one side of the swingarm (the right side in this case) was a new feature for Japanese manufacturers. The U-joint was a miniature version of a regular car type, protected by a rubber boot, but without any grease provision for the needle roller bearing assemblies. There was a BMW-type spiral bevel gear rear drive unit, although the pinion shaft had Timkin-type tapered roller bearings rather than the BMW's ball bearings, but this also lacked a

grease fitting. It was necessary to pull out the entire rear end to grease the splines every 6,000 miles (10,000km). Even then, grease was sometimes expelled from the tight-fitting splines, permitting them to rust as condensation could collect in the unvented housing. As most owners neglected to perform this maintenance chore there were cases of driveline failure on some 1975 Gold Wings. Fortunately this problem was rectified for 1976, and could be retro-fitted to those first K0 Gold Wings. Driveshaft lubrication aside, one of the other problems was the exceptionally high gearing provided by the 3.40:1 final drive. This saw the engine remain in the lowest quarter of its rev range most of the time and was an impediment if attaching a sidecar or towing a trailer. It was not long though before the aftermarket provided lower-ratio final drives, generally a 4.0:1.

As with the BMW there was a spring-loaded shock absorber incorporated into the driveshaft. This was another time-honoured feature that Honda had perfected for their flagship, its origins going back to the primary drive shock absorbers in pre-war British singles. The swingarm itself pivoted on needle bearings, a much more effective system than Honda's usual plastic bushes. All these features indicated Honda's intention to create a machine of exceptional quality. However, while the driveshaft may have been functional, simple practical features such as easy rear wheel removal to repair a puncture or change a tyre were overlooked. Rear wheel removal required lowering of the exhaust system but other maintenance tasks were easier than on most other motorcycles. As the cylinder heads were easily accessible, valve adjustment by screw and locknut was straightforward. Routine maintenance called for periodic timing belt replacement, but no more so than with a comparable car. When it came to the ignition system the Gold Wing again exhibited conservatism. Unlike other companies at that

Setting the Gold Wing apart from the Harley-Davidson Electra Glide was its shaft final drive. This 1976 Limited Edition has gold-anodised alloy wheel rims. (Roy Kidney)

time, Honda resisted experimentation with an electronic CDI system, and the Gold Wing relied on the tried and tested battery, points and coils. Two sets of points (each firing two cylinders) were located under a cover on the rear of the left cylinder head. Again more easily accessible than on some other machines. The mechanical ignition advance provided 10° up until 650–800rpm, with a maximum of 23–24.5°. For all its clever engineering though, the Gold Wing engine needed to last a long time. Compared with the average motorcycle engine this wasn't an easy engine to repair or overhaul, but fortunately for motorcycle mechanics everywhere, overhauls were rarely required.

Honda certainly achieved their design criteria with the Gold Wing, but the actual performance of the engine surprised many. Unlike most touring motorcycles the Gold Wing just didn't provide adequate low and mid-range power and

it was only outperformed by one other motorcycle in 1975, Kawasaki's 903cc Z1. The Z1 made 82bhp, and weighed 45kg (100lb) less, but the Gold Wing almost matched it even on the dragstrip and in top speed. Despite the upright riding position the Gold Wing was capable of nearly 130mph (210kph).

The chassis

As with the engine there was little revolutionary about the chassis specifications, but some of the features too were innovative for a touring motorcycle. By 1975 front disc brakes had only recently superseded drums, but a rear disc was almost a novelty. Only a handful of highly specified and expensive limited edition Italian machines then came with a rear disc brake, but

In 1975 rear disc brakes were rare on motorcycles, as were 17-inch wheels with large-section tyres. (Roy Kidney)

its appearance on the Gold Wing made it seem conventional. The stainless steel rear disc too was a large, 295mm (11.6in) in diameter, with a dual opposed piston brake caliper. This was almost in contrast to the front brakes that were smaller stainless steel twin discs (273mm/10.75in) riveted to alloy carriers, with single floating piston brake calipers. Rather than mounting on a swinging arm like the brake calipers of the CB 750, the Gold Wing front calipers had guide pins to allow for lateral movement to compensate for pad wear. Compared with a dual opposed piston design though they were still inferior, and prone to seizure through corrosion. While it seemed strange to place a larger, higher specification braking system on the rear, this too was to

strongly influence the general specification of motorcycles for many years to come. Even BMW later succumbed to fitting larger rear discs than those on the front. One feature though that was quite innovative was the location of the front calipers behind the fork legs rather than in front. All disc-braked motorcycles at that time featured forward-mounted brake calipers but it made more sense to mount them behind to get the weight closer to the steering centreline to reduce steering inertia. There was also a practical benefit in that the front wheel was also more easily removed for tyre changes.

Also reflecting the quality of the Gold Wing were the wire-spoked wheels with lightweight aluminium rims. This emphasis on reducing unsprung weight seemed almost unnecessary given the large overall weight but was indicative of Honda's detailing. Unfortunately these wheels were to prove a weak point in the specification and prone to failure. The power and weight of the Gold Wing, especially a fully loaded one, was often too much for the spokes, particularly on the rear; 17-inch wheels were relatively unusual at that time, and the wide (2.50in) aluminium rim was cleverly designed with a square section hollowed around each side of the rim's bead area to minimise weight. Unfortunately there were no security bolts or rim screws to retain the tyre in the event of a puncture. Of more concern was the design of the spokes themselves. These were not a stronger straight pull design but a weaker bent type, almost being positioned vertically as the rear hub was even narrower than that of the CB 750. It was no surprise that these wheels only lasted for three years and were replaced by Comstars in 1978. Unfortunately though, the Comstars were not that much better, best being remembered as one of Honda's less satisfactory experiments. The front wheel was the standard 1.85 x 19-inch of the period, this almost looking too small on the large Gold Wing.

In an era where skinny front forks

predominated, Honda took the step of increasing the fork leg diameter to 37mm (up from 35mm on the CB 750). To further increase rigidity there were also four clamping bolts underneath each fork leg for the axle. The large chromed front mudguard also featured rubber blocks so as not to contribute to fork binding. The forks provided a reasonable 143mm (5.63in) of travel. At the rear were rather limp twin shock absorbers, adjustable only for spring preload and giving 86.3mm (3.4in) of travel. The frame too was a conventional tubular steel duplex full cradle type, providing an unremarkable 28° of fork angle. It was also the attention to detail that set the Gold Wing apart. Features such as an audible indicator alarm, and a starter motor which cut out unless the clutch was engaged if the machine was in gear. While on other motorcycles the rider had to search around for the choke lever, on the Gold Wing this was conveniently placed on the instrument panel. On that first Gold Wing the instrument faces were dark green, with a coolant gauge incorporated in the tachometer. There was a choice of two colours, Candy Antares Red or Candy Blue Green.

Certainly, the Gold Wing rewrote the book regarding acceptable size and weight of a mainstream motorcycle. The wet weight of 293.5kg (647lb) was considerably more than any other motorcycle of that time except the Harley-Davidson FLH 1200. But that weight was extremely cleverly disguised by the flat-four engine layout which provided a low centre of gravity. More significant than the weight though

The Gold Wing came with dual front disc brakes with rear-mounted single-piston brake calipers. All the power and weight tested the skinny front forks to the limit. (Roy Kidney)

was the gross vehicle weight rating of 461kg (1,015lb). Although this really allowed for only 163kg (360lb) above the wet weight, it was a more generous allowance than provided by most other touring motorcycles. It was only in the practical areas of seating and suspension compliance that the Gold Wing showed evidence of being designed by engineers rather than motorcyclists. The seat was too hard, especially for long trips, and the suspension lacked compliance over small bumps. It was stiffly sprung, probably to maintain straight line stability when heavily loaded up – and being loaded up was what the Gold Wing was really about with two whole pages devoted to 'Accessories and Loading' in the owners' manual. Honda had undeniably created a showstopper. This was a motorcycle that was impossible to ignore, and one about which nearly everyone, not just motorcyclists, had an opinion.

Magazine opinion of the Gold Wing was divided around the world. Here is an early version on test by *Two Wheels* magazine in Australia. Here, unlike in the UK, the outcome was extremely favourable. (*Two Wheels*)

Impact: the two-wheeled car –

or a gigantic step forward?

Amid a blaze of public relations hype there was little doubt that the Gold Wing would cause a stir when it was released. Launched with slogans varying from 'the epitome of what touring is all about', and 'the most advanced motorcycle ever made', the Gold Wing met with generally more favourable acclaim in the USA than in Europe. Here was a machine that immediately polarised opinion. For many conservative, and more sporting orientated, motorcyclists the Gold Wing seemed excessive. Yet even these detractors couldn't deride the efficiency of the Gold Wing as a single-purpose touring motorcycle. They countered that despite its obviously brilliant engineering and refinement it was too big and heavy to be taken seriously for anything other than interstate cruising. To these people the Gold Wing seemed overly complex with its myriad of electrical components and was nothing more than a two-wheeled car. Motorcyclists in America who rode the highways however, respected the Gold Wing for what it could do that no other machine could. Even non-motorcyclists, and those with no knowledge of motorcycling, were impressed by the Gold Wing. For the first time a

motorcycle transcended boundaries and this was the first motorcycle to represent many traditional American automotive features. The Gold Wing was large, roomy, powerful, reliable, easy to live with, and above all, packed with features. This made it appealing to a whole new world of riders, many who may not even have considered a motorcycle previously.

The detractors complained that many of the features of the Gold Wing were unnecessary. Were motorcycles with electric fuel pumps and indicator beepers really indispensable? How times change. Twenty-five years on that first Gold Wing seems almost simple and small, even compared with some of the latest so-called sporting offerings from Japan. While it may not have been revolutionary, the Gold Wing was undoubtedly a visionary motorcycle. So much so that there are few designs in production that share as many similarities with a 25-year-old original.

To gain maximum publicity Honda cleverly released the machine separately in various markets around the world. With the United States really being the core market for the Gold Wing, it was shown to the US press soon after the Cologne Show, at a dealer convention in

Las Vegas. A prototype Gold Wing caused such a favourable impression that it was inevitable that press reports would be positive. When the first full road test appeared in *Cycle* magazine in April 1975, they applauded the Gold Wing as the most focused design for a touring motorcycle yet produced. What was particularly surprising was the performance. A standing start quarter mile time of 12.92 seconds at 104.52mph (168kph) placed the Gold Wing well and truly in the Superbike category. Only a month later, in May 1975, the venerable Bob Greene tested the Gold Wing for *Motorcyclist*, but he was less euphoric and saw the machine as a new extension of the touring concept. Rather then replacing existing touring machines Greene saw the Gold Wing as complementary.

It was one thing testing the Gold Wing on its own, but in August 1975 *Cycle* pitted it against seven competitive touring motorcycles over a gruelling month and a half period. This was a more realistic appraisal and the test included the two motorcycles that had influenced the design of the Gold Wing the most: the BMW R90/6 and Harley-Davidson FLH 1200. Other machines vying for touring honours were Suzuki's new RE-5 Rotary, the older GT-750M, the Kawasaki Z-1B, Moto Guzzi's 850T, and another relic from the past, the Norton 850 Interstate. That the brand new Gold Wing tied with the well-developed BMW R90/6 for first place said much for the excellence of Honda's design approach. It was also no surprise that the ageing Harley finished last in almost every functional comparative category. The BMW and Gold Wing were clearly the most outstanding tourers, but whereas the BMW was the result of many years of refinement the Gold Wing was a fresh design, and could only improve with further development.

While the US testers appreciated the refinement and quality of the Gold Wing, in Britain there was more cynicism. The British press launch was at the Isle of Man TT in June 1975 and this probably wasn't the ideal location to release such a motorcycle. The Gold Wing received a mixed reaction from that Isle of Man launch, not only being termed a two-wheeled car, but also coined the 'Lead Wing'. Probably the most significant test in the UK was Bill Haylock's in *Bike* magazine, in January 1976. It wasn't so much that Haylock's test was the only test in a British magazine, it was more that Haylock was so sceptical that it is the one road test that has been remembered. As an owner and aficionado of the tiny sporting Ducati 450 desmo single, Haylock seemed more concerned about the direction that Japanese motorcycles were taking than assessing the competence of the Gold Wing as a touring motorcycle. Given the subsequent success of the Gold Wing and the demise of the Ducati single, Bill Haylock was undoubtedly out of touch with reality. However, despite Honda withdrawing their advertising from *Bike* and refusing to supply test bikes for over a year, the magazine had such a large circulation that this test may have affected the acceptance of the Gold Wing in the British market. This still didn't stop frame specialists Dresda Autos of London developing a chassis for the GL 1000 at the request of Honda UK Ltd executive Ken Hull. With cast alloy wheels, S&W rear suspension, and twin Lockheed front brakes, this was only lightly tuned and entered in the 1976 Formula One TT at the Isle of Man. In the hands of Hugh Evans the machine astounded the critics by turning in 90mph (145kph) laps with a top speed around 155mph (250kph) before retiring in the race with a broken oil pressure relief valve. At an earlier outing at Thruxton the crankshaft broke. A Gold Wing was even developed for endurance racing by the Swiss Honda importer during 1976. This had a specially constructed steel

Gold Wing associations and clubs

The acceptance of the Gold Wing may have been slower than Honda expected, but it wasn't long before it became acknowledged as the only really serious touring motorcycle. The original Gold Wing became something of a legend in its own lifetime, and June 1977 saw the formation of what is now the largest single-marque motorcycle organisation in the world, the Gold Wing Road Riders Association (GWRRA). Seven enthusiasts got together in search of a 'family Gold Wing organisation' that would provide increased membership benefits over conventional motorcycle clubs, without the usual restrictive attendance regulations. Considering that most one-make clubs were centred on deceased or British marques at that time the establishment of a Gold Wing owners' group was indicative of the uniqueness of the machine's appeal. Based in Phoenix, Arizona, by 1981 the membership was already 6,000, increasing to 18,000 by 1983. In 23 years the GWRRA has grown to include more than 70,000 members in 52 countries and is the second largest motorcycle club in the world (after the Harley Owners Group). With a motto 'Friends for Fun, Safety and Knowledge', the association is non-profit, non-religious, and non-political. It is also influential, and Honda only released the GL 1100 Interstate in 1980 as a result of direct liaison with the GWRRA.

Undoubtedly the success of the organisation is that it offers a unique experience and accepts people from all walks of life and with varied interests and backgrounds. Members join the Gold Wing family and 1,000 active Chapters, managed by 4,000 volunteers foster this. There is no typical Gold Wing owner, and ownership of a Gold Wing transcends the normal boundaries associated with motorcycles. The emphasis in the GWRRA is as a family organisation, and this includes restaurant runs, picnic rides, campouts, charity runs and parades. There is also a strong emphasis on safety within the organisation and many members have completed first aid training and safety workshops. Membership of the GWRRA not only allows Gold Wing owners to enjoy camaraderie and friendship, there is a huge resource of technical and practical assistance available. This ranges from tow assistance to the huge *Gold Book* directory. This lists participating members' names and telephone numbers with details of the assistance they can provide, be it lodging or simply friendship.

In addition to the GWRRA, the Indianapolis-based Gold Wing Touring Association offers a similar service with individual Chapters and a 'Destination Friendship' motto. For American Gold Wing owners there is also the American Gold Wing Association, this being created in 1983 as an AMA Charterer organisation totally manned by volunteers. This also fosters a similar desire for fun, fellowship and safety with a family emphasis. The Gold Wing European Federation comprises membership from 18 nations and includes over 10,000 members. Affiliated with this is the Gold Wing Owners Club GB. Harry Ward began this in May 1980 with 37 members following the arrival of a 24-strong contingent of Wing Nuts from the UK at a Gold Wing rally in Belgium. One of the most active motorcycle clubs in Britain, this has expanded to include around 2,000 members, with 37 regional sections. Even owners of older Gold Wings have a specific club, Carl Hinsey's Classic Wing Club catering purely for owners of 1975–79 GL 1000s.

Part of the key to the success of the Gold Wing and the Gold Wing Road Riders Association has been its appeal to a new, and often older, group of riders. Typical Gold Wing riders are Charlie and Joan Sento, with a high-mileage GL 1200. (*Cycle World*)

For Southern Californian optician Lonnie Casper this 1989 GL 1500 was his only mode of transport. With his wife Linda they have covered around 30,000 miles a year. (*Cycle World*)

frame and rising rate monoshock rear suspension system by Pierre Doncque who was also responsible for the all-conquering Godier-Genoud Kawasakis. However, while the racing Gold Wings looked small and sleek compared with the in-line four-cylinder competition, at 230kg (507lb) they were too heavy. The three-bearing crankshaft was also not strong enough for the demands of continuous high rpm, although the Honda Suisse Gold Wing of Burki and Fourgeaud managed a surprising fifth place in the 1976 Liège 24-hour race in Belgium.

In Australia, often a market representing an amalgam of the US and Britain, *Two Wheels* magazine in July 1975 claimed the Gold Wing to be 'the most significant new model in motorcycling in a decade!' They concluded that while the Honda may not sell as many as the CB 750, 'the introduction of the model marks an even more significant milestone. Quite suddenly motorcycling has taken a gigantic step forward.'

What most of the journalistic detractors failed to see was that the market, particularly in the USA, wanted the Gold Wing. Wing riders were older and more experienced than the average motorcyclist and probably didn't read motorcycle magazines anyway. They also rode their motorcycles more and had a higher disposable income. It wasn't only the high price of the machine in the first place, but nearly every Gold Wing owner would then spend considerably more on accessories. US Wing owners (or Wing Nuts) were typically white-collar middle class in their forties, although in Europe the average owner was slightly younger and less affluent. Thus it was no coincidence that Gold Wing sales in the USA were significantly more than in Europe. The requirements for a touring motorcycle in Europe were markedly different to those in America so the Gold Wing would always be a

Living with an early GL 1000 and GL 1100

There is no doubt that over the past 25 years the Gold Wing has been one of Honda's most reliable models. It arrived at a time when Honda had a somewhat dubious reputation for producing engines that ate camshafts and camchains. All the CB-series of singles, twins and fours suffered and in the early 1970s mechanics seemed busy fixing CB125s, 250s, 360s, and even the 400, 550, and 750cc fours. The next generation of twins (250 and 400 Dreams and CX 500) and double overhead camshaft fours were also problematic, so the Gold Wing was like a breath of fresh air to Honda mechanics.

Although initially ridiculed as a 'two-wheeled car' by some, it was purely the automotive influence that led to the vastly improved engine reliability of the Gold Wing. The engine would last far longer than 100,000 miles (160,000km) even on standard pistons and rings, and often it was the ancillary components that would fail before the engine. As with all motors with toothed-rubber timing belts it was important to maintain these correctly. However, as so many variables affect timing belt wear Honda didn't provide

The Gold Wing has always lent itself to customisation, as evidenced by this three-wheeled 'trike' created out of an early GL 1000. (Ian Falloon)

recommended maintenance intervals until 1996. They then began recommending an 'inspect and clean' for the belts at a very conservative 100,000 miles. Generally most Honda servicing departments suggest inspection and adjustment at around 15,000

Popular additions to the GL 1000 were a Vetter Windjammer fairing and saddlebags, as fitted to this 1978 GL 1000. (Roy Kidney)

IMPACT:THE TWO-WHEELED CAR

As Honda improved the Gold Wing annually owners set out to individualise their machines with even more determination. Here is a 1980 GL 1100 with a cowboy look. (Roy Kidney)

miles with replacement at approximately 60,000 miles. As excessive heat can destroy rubber belts prematurely it is essential that the cooling system is operating effectively. The consequences of timing belt failure can be catastrophic as the lower end of the engine continues to turn with a static top end. Even though there were annual improvements, some GL 1100s were known to develop a noisy growl in the rear of the motor that seemed difficult to eliminate.

When it came to living with an early GL 1000 on a day-to-day basis one of the most irritating components was the contact breaker ignition system. This was blamed for misfiring under load and spark

plug failure and was particularly prone to wear. Many owners fitted an electronic ignition set-up (Dyna S, Piranha, Boyer Bransden or similar). Not only were the points problematic but the coils too were weak. Another problem besetting high mileage GL 1000s is rocker wear. The overall gearing on 1975 until 1977 Gold wings was also too high for most applications, and exacerbated if fitted with a sidecar or towing a trailer. Thus a popular aftermarket addition was a lower final drive gear set, this lowering the final drive from 3.4:1 to 4.0:1. At the expense of slightly heavier fuel consumption the GL 1000 could now overtake without downshifting, and climb hills more easily in top gear.

No matter what the press thought of the Gold Wing in a brief test, it was taken to heart with alacrity by the long distance touring crowd in the United States. Not only did owners start clocking up huge mileages, but also they soon found the standard machine wanting

Even with the release of the Interstate and its factory-fitted touring equipment the demand for aftermarket accessories grew. However, most additions were cosmetic rather than functional as seen on this GL 1100 Interstate with its chrome-plated brake covers. (Roy Kidney)

in terms of touring comfort. Surveys showed that up to 90 per cent of Gold Wings were equipped with some sort of touring fairing, but accessories didn't finish there. Soon there was a range of custom saddles, radios, floorboards, saddlebags, and even trailers available. When the Gold Wing was released factory-fitted fairings just didn't exist except on a small number of exclusive European sports bikes. There didn't seem any reason for the Japanese to compete with the likes of established aftermarket fairing suppliers such as Vetter or Luftmeister. Although Honda indicated shortly after the Gold Wing was released that fairings and saddlebags would soon be offered as official accessories, it wasn't until 1979 that their own bags became available. As expected this set of saddlebags and rear box was excellent quality, but their delay in appearing left the door open for a large number of independent suppliers to fill the void for several years. Honda were even slower to release a fairing for the Gold Wing, this not being available officially until 1980, with the release of the GL 1100 Interstate. In the meantime, a huge aftermarket industry grew.

Early Gold Wings were noted for their flat, hard, and uncomfortable dual seat, allowing a huge aftermarket to offer custom designed two-tier king-and-queen seats. As one observer opined 'Japanese seat no fit American backside'. Even when the factory provided improved seats in 1977, then again in 1978 and 1980, custom seats continued to sell. It wasn't until the GL 1100 that Honda finally provided an acceptable seat. Along with the seat, many early Gold Wing owners complained of the handlebars being too far forward. However, simply changing the bars wasn't as easy as it looked on the early versions as they had the handlebar switch wiring routed through the bars themselves. Aftermarket set-backs, complete with a Gold Wing insignia, soon became *de rigueur* for the Gold Wing owner.

Another area of complaint was the Showa suspension, at least until the 1980 model. The Gold Wing emerged right in the middle of the era where Japanese designers concentrated on engine development at the expense of chassis and suspension design and the Gold Wing epitomised this more than most. The front fork springs were intentionally stiff, to maintain adequate ground clearance for the wide flat-four engine, but provided such a high degree of static friction (stiction) that they barely responded to minor road irregularities such as highway expansion joints. On top of that the 37mm fork legs were not stiff enough for such a large

motorcycle and suffered from fore and aft flex under braking as well as providing an extremely harsh ride. Owners of early Gold Wings could experiment with different fork oil and fork springs (Progressive) but it wasn't until the GL 1100 appeared in 1980 with air suspension that the problem was satisfactorily resolved.

The rear suspension was no better. Too soft, they allowed the rear end to wallow unnervingly in corners as well as bottoming out too easily and contributing little to ride comfort. They also suffered premature fade and were often useless after only 4,000 miles. Inevitably the aftermarket leapt at the opportunity to offer replacement rear shock absorbers and soon Gold Wings were seen with alternatives from a variety of manufacturers including Progressive, Koni, Girling, Boge-Mulholland and S&W. Other functional accessories included additional pannier fuel tanks to increase the rather meagre touring range, and

chrome exhaust systems to replace the rust-prone original, 1975–77 system. For those owners seeking an increase in chassis stiffness both fork braces and reinforced swingarms were available, and Lester soon produced cast alloy wheels as a bolt-on replacement for the wire-spoked items.

Even by 1976 the tailor-made aftermarket accessory industry for the Gold Wing was well underway. Beyond the functional accessories Wing dressing moved into an art form as owners added engine protection bars, floorboards, exhaust extensions, and an array of chrome-plated accessories from timing belt covers to saddlebag rails. As Honda continued to respond to criticisms by offering annual improvements, the aftermarket industry expanded by offering an even wider variety of custom accessories. As a result the Gold Wing just became more entrenched as the leading touring motorcycle available.

Not content with chrome plating, many components on this GL 1100 Interstate are *gold* plated. (Roy Kidney)

minority machine. In the USA the Gold Wing was often a first-time motorcycle, bought by those whose kids had grown up. A Gold Wing gave them the opportunity to explore the country and recapture their lost youth. Touring on a motorcycle also appealed to a rebellious side of their nature. This was something their parents wouldn't have allowed them to do and while early sales figures may have been below expectations, soon Honda was selling around 25,000 Gold Wings each year.

Because of the more responsible nature of owners, the Gold Wing has done much to promote an improved community attitude to motorcycles. As most Gold Wings are beautifully presented, and quiet, they have provided the general public with a more positive side to the pursuit of motorcycling. There was something different about the Gold Wing, something that set it and its riders apart from other motorcyclists, but they were still motorcycles. Then of course there is the ego of the Gold Wing rider. He or she wants to be noticed and consequently most Gold Wings are decked out to reflect the owner's personality.

Evolution: 1,000 to 1,100cc

Although the first-year sales of only 5,000 were well under the forecast 60,000, it was significant that 4,000 of these were in the USA. The Gold Wing was well on the way to being accepted in that primary market and for 1976 the model was essentially unchanged, but for cosmetics and an important driveshaft development. Under the leadership of Einosuke Miyachi, the Gold Wing development team added an external grease nipple to the front of the rear driveshaft housing, enabling easy lubrication of the coupling. They also incorporated an internal seal to keep the grease on the splines. Greasing was still required at 6,000-mile (10,000km) intervals but this was a lot simpler than removing the driveshaft as had been required earlier. Other changes for 1976 included a wiper on the oil level sight window, a carburettor link guard and two helmet holders. Cosmetically, Sulphur Yellow replaced green as a main colour and the instrument faces were light green. After one year though the Gold Wing was beginning to be accepted by touring riders, particularly in the USA.

In addition to the basic GL 1000 K1, there was also the GL 1000 LTD Gold Wing Limited Edition for 1976. Only produced in Custom Candy Brown, this featured gold anodised wheel rims with gold-coloured spokes, gold emblems and striping, and a chrome-plated

Apart from a new colour of Sulphur Yellow there were few changes to the Gold Wing for 1976. The hard seat remained so most owners fitted a more comfortable aftermarket unit. (Roy Kidney)

One of the changes for 1976 was light green faces on the Nippon Denso instruments. (Roy Kidney)

radiator shield. The LTD also received a dual contoured seat and a special tool kit in a leather-type bag. Other detail touches included a gold-stamped owners' manual, a leather key case, and a slightly flared front mudguard. Available only in the USA, and at a premium price of $3,295, it was a particularly handsome machine, and with only 2,000 produced it is quite a rarity nowadays. The British importer,

Honda (UK) Ltd, also jumped on the limited edition bandwagon in 1976, although on a much smaller scale. To promote a prestigious image for the slow-selling Gold Wing they had the well-known British accessory supplier Rickman produce 52 Gold Wing Executives, one for each week of the year. Setting the Executive apart from the regular Gold Wing was a black finish, frame-mounted Rickman

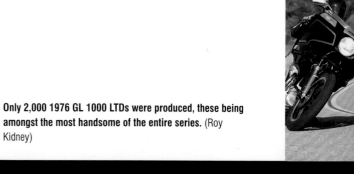

Only 2,000 1976 GL 1000 LTDs were produced, these being amongst the most handsome of the entire series. (Roy Kidney)

Special features on the Limited Edition included a dual-contoured seat and gold emblems and striping. The brown paint was fashionable at that time. (Roy Kidney)

fairing, engine protection bars and rear rack, and American-made Lester cast-aluminium wheels.

There was a new team leader for 1977, Masaru Shirakura, who had previously been involved in the development of smaller models, in particular the 125–175cc range. This year the GL 1000 K2 model saw a few more detail modifications, notably to improve comfort and reduce noise. This included a dual-contoured seat, and 67mm higher and recontoured handlebars with neoprene handgrips instead of the earlier plastic waffle-type. The handlebars came in for some criticism as being too high and far forward and handlebar set-backs continued as popular aftermarket items. The steering head now featured tapered roller bearings instead of the earlier wear-prone balls, and the exhaust header pipes received chrome covers to hide the black-painted finish. The upper engine mounting brackets were also chrome and the fuel tank specially treated to prevent rust. A development to the clutch saw both the steel plates now carrying the power, but this still didn't solve all the clutch problems. Further noise reduction saw thicker engine casings, with the rear engine and cylinder head increasing from 2.5 to 4mm, and the front engine cover thickness increasing from 2.5 to 3mm. New colours also appeared for 1977, Candy Sirus Blue and black joining the red. The tank now featured more pinstriping and the instrument faces were black, with green kph markings.

The year 1978 saw the first major revisions of the Gold Wing, with the appearance of the GL 1000 K3. There was another project leader, Masahiro Senbu, and he set out to address some of the earlier complaints. These included a lack of low-end and mid-range power, comfort, and wet-weather braking. Thus there were significant changes to the wheels, instruments, seat and engine. While there was

For 1977 there were higher handlebars and an improved
seat, but the black-painted exhaust system remained.
(*Cycle*)

also new styling, most of the radical
development was to the engine.

The earlier engine had been a strong
dragstrip performer, but was noticeably
anaemic in top gear acceleration for rapid
overtaking. Thus for 1978 there were slightly
smaller (31mm) Keihin constant vacuum
carburettors, shorter valve timing, and more
ignition advance. The valve timing provided 15°
less intake duration, the inlet valve now closing
35° after bottom dead centre, and 10° less
exhaust duration with the exhaust valve
opening 40° before bottom dead centre.
Ignition advance was still 10° until 650–800rpm,
but now increased to a maximum of 25.5–27°.
Despite retaining the tall gearing, the engine
response was significantly improved, although
the claimed power was reduced slightly to
78hp. Another engine development was aimed
at reducing the clouds of smoke that would
emanate after starting following being parked
on the sidestand for any period. This was due
to oil from the crankcase leaking down the left

cylinder and into the combustion chamber
through ring gaps in the oil ring. Locating rings
were added to the oil ring grooves to keep the
ring gap at the top of the cylinder, effectively
overcoming this annoying problem. Further
engine developments included a spring-loaded
floating bar primary drive tensioner rather than
the earlier model's stationary primary chain
guide. Given the emphasis on improving
general rideability, it was strange that the GL
1000 K3 was fitted with extremely cold Nippon
Denso X24ESU spark plugs. These contributed
to hesitancy at small throttle openings, and
with lean EPA carburettor jetting the engine
remained cold-blooded. Installation of warmer
extended electrode Champion A-8Y-MC spark
plugs could alleviate this problem. US
Environmental Protection Agency (EPA)
requirements also saw the crankcase breather
feeding into the airbox rather than the
atmosphere.

Completing the engine changes was a new
exhaust system, now fully chromed, with two

The first major revisions to the GL 1000 occurred for 1978. The wheels were now Comstar, and the exhaust system was chromed. (American Honda)

smaller mufflers replacing the giant U-shaped muffler/balance pipe of earlier Gold Wings. Not only did these pipes make a better sound (it was felt the early Wings were too quiet), but they looked better and allowed easier access to the clutch. As the clutch was still one of the weaknesses in the drivetrain this was welcomed. Also deleted finally was the unnecessary kickstart.

It wasn't only the engine that came in for some attention. Comfort was improved through some changes to the suspension. The front fork delivered 25mm (1in) more travel and had springs 6mm longer. Damping was improved

through increasing the size and number of holes in the damper rods, and static friction was reduced with chamfers cut into the bottom of the fork tubes to channel oil between the tubes and sliders. At the rear were new FVQ shock absorbers with two-stage damping. While the suspension compliance was improved, the forks were still some way from being as effective as those on the latest Yamahas and Suzukis, and the FVQ shocks soon gained the nickname 'Fade Very Quickly'.

Complaints about the wet weather braking performance of earlier Gold Wings saw the US Department of Transportation investigate the

Production in America

With more than 80 per cent of Gold Wing production heading to the USA it was inevitable that Honda would eventually look at creating a motorcycle production plant there. However, when Honda decided in 1977 to build a plant in Marysville, Ohio, a small town in America's Midwest and home to only 7,500 inhabitants, it seemed incredulous. During the 1970s, American-made products gained a poor reputation amongst consumers and Honda set about to change this with the Marysville Motorcycle Plant. Honda needed the US plant to succeed if it was to expand into automotive manufacture and with typical determination Honda proceeded with their plan, and both Marysville and Honda have benefited considerably since.

At a cost of $50 million, the Marysville Motorcycle Plant opened on 10 June 1979. Only ten motorcycles (built by 64 employees) were manufactured on that first day. The 260,000sq ft Marysville plant provided a capacity for the production of 60,000 motorcycles a year. It was initially devoted to the Elsinore CR 250R being joined later in 1979 by the CBX 1000 with Gold Wing production starting in 1980 with the new GL 1100. Finally, the Gold Wing became what it was really all along, an American motorcycle. Within three months the Marysville Motorcycle Plant was so successful that the construction of a Honda automobile manufacturing plant was also sanctioned. Apart from some early problems with American suppliers due to the low production numbers of only 150 Gold Wings a day from 1981 until 1983 (compared with 1,000 a day in Japan) production proceeded smoothly. Honda's policy of local hiring and spreading the work meant that only one person per family could work at the Marysville plant, and only those living within a 30-mile radius were considered for employment. Working at the Honda plant was considered so desirable that many workers moved to Marysville, and employment took place after three exhaustive interviews.

Initially though, most parts of the Gold Wing were still manufactured in Japan and assembled in Marysville with a selection of US-manufactured items. By 1985, the fairings and saddlebags were injection moulded on the premises, and the tank stampings welded and painted. The frames were built by robots. More American contribution was evident with the completion of a new engine plant in nearby Anna, Ohio, in 1985. Here, all the casting, forging, machining, and heat-treating processes were undertaken in the one plant. The success of these Honda of America plants was largely due to the way the Japanese corporate philosophy was translated to the small town in America's Midwest. Workers were called 'associates', and while they didn't share the lifetime employment benefits enjoyed by their oriental counterparts, they operated in a spirit of cooperation with the managers. Dressed in identical white smocks they showed a commitment to product quality often lacking in other American manufacturing plants. Associates were offered a single pay scale for all assembly processes, facilitating movement between departments, and contributing to high job satisfaction. Open communication existed, with all associates being treated equally, right down to all employees sharing a common lunchroom. If there was any criticism that could be levelled at Marysville's employees it was that they could have been producing anything; they just happened to make motorcycles. It was intended to build a domed, climate-controlled test facility next to the Marysville plant so as to be able to undertake testing even throughout the rather severe Ohio winter. Ultimately the project was scrapped due to the cost, but Honda had already planted special grass that would survive under the dome.

Building a Gold Wing took about the same time as to assemble a Honda Civic car 2½ hours. 65 associates were involved in the assembly that took place through a series of 34 assembly line processes. Each process was timed to 300 seconds, with 10 to 15 individual tasks completed within that period. Carrying around 2,000 parts, a completed Gold Wing comprised as many components as a four-door Honda Accord. Following the success of the Marysville plant Honda has expanded their production capacity to include seven other manufacturing plants. While motorcycles have gradually become less important in the overall Honda corporate picture, Marysville continues to assemble Gold Wings, but for *awhile*, the six-cylinder engine production moved to the nearby Anna plant, Ohio. The one-millionth US-built Honda left the Marysville production line on 26 July 1996. It was of course a Gold Wing.

In January 2000, the Marysville plant was completely redesigned to enable production of the new GL 1800. Two new bays were added to the weld shop, and 16 welding machines to handle the GL 1800's aluminium frame. The paint shop required new fixtures for the plastic body parts, along with 14 new sets of dies for the 23 body parts. A new chassis dyno was installed at the end of the production line to test the anti-lock braking system. To improve quality many of Marysville's associates travelled to Honda's Hamamatsu facility in Japan to study manufacturing processes. The emphasis was on providing the highest standard of fit and finish. The other major change was in the move of engine production from Anna back to Marysville, and the first GL 1800 rolled off the production line on 10 October 2000.

An associate works on a GL 1800 as it nears completion on
the Marysville production line. (American Honda)

Gold Wing during 1977. Surprisingly it wasn't the front brake performance, but the rear disc that saw a recall of all Gold Wings prior to 1978. The recall involved fitting grooved pads of different material. Thus there were new discs and brake calipers for the K3 model. The discs came from the CB 750 F2, and were not only thinner and lighter, but were claimed to provide better efficiency while wet. With the new brakes came Honda's patented multi-piece Comstar wheels. While all other manufacturers were moving towards more rigid cast aluminium wheels, Honda decided to go for a wheel with designed-in flex. The Comstar featured an aluminium rim bolted to pressed aluminium spokes but it was soon discovered that the aluminium spokes were insufficiently strong to cope with the weight of the Gold Wing, so wheels with steel spokes soon replaced these. The rim and tyre sizes remained unchanged with the K3.

Completing the specification for 1978 was a totally revised instrument layout. Not only were the main dials black, with red kph markings, but there was an additional instrument panel mounted on an inclined panel built into the top of the storage housing of the dummy fuel tank. This included water temperature, a wildly pessimistic fuel gauge, and a voltmeter. There were now twin horns (an automotive-type, high and low), a redesigned centre and side stand, and the rear turn signals relocated to the rear fender allowing for the easier fitting of saddlebags.

Along with another new seat, there were also new colours, with black joining Candy Limited Maroon and Candy Grandeur Blue. The result of all these changes saw the dry weight increase to 273kg (601lb), this also seeing a drop in performance. *Cycle* magazine now managed a standing start quarter mile in 13.38 seconds at 98.90mph (159kph) in their test of a GL 1000 K3 in March 1978. After three years

the Gold Wing was beginning to suffer in comparison with some of the newer Japanese touring models, particularly Yamaha's shaft-drive XS 1100. The Yamaha was more comfortable, faster, lighter, had better handling, and offered a greater carrying capacity.

Despite the K3 needing a serious overhaul to enable it to better the Yamaha XS 1100, this would have to wait until 1980. In the meantime, there was a new development team leader, Ryo Nashimoto, but the K4 for 1979 received only detail changes. These included rectangular turn signals and brake fluid reservoir (instead of the earlier round type), black anodised levers and a new twin-bulb taillight with CBX 1000-type ribbed lens, with all models receiving the 60/55-watt quartz halogen headlight. One-piece brake discs made their way back, with ten supporting spokes instead of five, but otherwise the K4 was much as before. The earlier black made way for Candy Burgundy and more than ever, the Gold Wing was looking in need of a makeover. In a comparison of six touring bikes by the US magazine *Motorcyclist* in June 1979, the Gold Wing came out as the loser with poor ride comfort, handling and throttle response, as well as excessive weight and a peaky powerband. Being last was not something that Honda was used to, and they set about redeeming themselves with alacrity.

The GL 1100

After five years with 999cc and only minimal development, 1980 saw the first milestone in the progress of the Gold Wing. Although it looked ostensibly like a big bore job on the earlier version, the GL 1100 was effectively an all-new motorcycle. It wasn't only the Yamaha XS 1100 that threatened the Gold Wing's domination of the touring market, with the advent of Kawasaki's six-cylinder Z1300 it was obvious that the Gold Wing needed more than just a facelift and a little extra displacement. With the GL 1100 Honda engineers achieved what they set out to do, and the earlier Gold Wing's shortcomings were eliminated.

With a new leader, Shuji Tanaka, the Gold Wing development team set out to answer many of the criticisms that had been levelled at the bike since 1975. In particular this included the seat and suspension, and annoying features such as the cold-bloodedness of the engine and the limited maximum load capacity. Tanaka was primarily a frame designer, working for the now defunct motorcycle producer Tohatsu before joining Honda in 1961. He was then involved in the frame design for a wide range of motorcycles, from the CB 90 to the CBX 1000. Coming to the Gold Wing with such impressive credentials, he was to head this project for five model years.

To cope with the added weight of fairings and accessories, the engine capacity was increased to 1,085cc through a 3mm overbore with 75mm pistons. The compression ratio remained at 9.2:1. However, there were many more changes to the engine than simply these larger pistons. In response to a small number of crankshaft breakages in Europe where Gold Wings were ridden at higher speeds than in America, the crankshaft was considerably stronger. The main bearing journals went up to 43mm and the con-rod journals to 46mm. With this increase the main/rod overlap went from 10.8mm to 13.8mm. Along with the stronger crankshaft came a 6mm wider Hy-Vo primary drive chain with a new set of tensioners. The primary chain now drove the clutch sprocket through softer, round cushions rather than the earlier wedge-shaped inserts. Considering the clutch problems the 999cc engine had suffered it was no surprise to see a completely new clutch on the GL 1100. The basket was now

cast aluminium rather than steel, with plates 7mm larger in diameter than before. Rather than the sandwich-type shock absorbing plate, there was a smaller three-piece bellows-type washer. There was also a revised clutch release mechanism, similar to that of the CBX 1000 six. This no longer used the earlier machined scrolling device with a ball and ramp, but relied instead on a simpler cam and cast lever. Completing the internal strengthening was an increase in the output shaft diameter to 28mm.

Although there were some minor emissions-related modifications to the piston and combustion chamber shape, more significant was another set of new camshafts. While the exhaust valve lift was unchanged at 8.5mm, the inlet valve lift increased slightly to 8.8mm. These camshafts also had new timing specifications. The inlet valve opened 5° before top dead centre, closing 43° after bottom dead centre, while the exhaust valve opened 45° before bottom dead centre, closing 5° after top dead centre. While the opening and closing points stayed the same, there was an increase of 8° in intake duration, and 5° for the exhaust. The valve sizes were 38mm for the inlet (up 1mm over the GL 1000) and 32mm for the exhaust (as before).

As longer duration camshafts were usually associated with narrower powerbands, Honda engineers countered this with smaller carburettors. Replacing the previous 31mm Keihins were four completely new aluminium-bodied Keihin constant-vacuum carburettors with 30mm throats. The smaller throats aided low speed running, and responsiveness improved through the installation of a single accelerator pump for the four carburettors. Each carburettor too now had its own air cut-out, anti-backfire valve. It had taken five years, but the Gold Wing also finally received electronic ignition with the GL 1100. Gone were the time-honoured points, these being replaced

Although undeniably a Gold Wing, there was much more to the 1980 GL 1100 than simply a larger engine. (*Cycle World*)

by a magnetic trigger. The ignition was still inductive, with the dual-lead coil's primary current being switched by an amplifier that received the signal from a pair of sensor coils over the crankshaft-driven reluctor. All the trigger components were now housed in the area previously occupied by the kickstart shaft so the earlier points chamber behind the left cylinder head was eliminated, providing further room for larger riders. There were now two ignition advance mechanisms; the centrifugal system of before that reduced the spark advance at low rpm, and an automotive-type vacuum advance that provided more spark lead at lighter throttle openings. This saw ignition advance increase from 37° before top dead centre to 50° to cure the earlier hesitation at low speeds.

Setting the new engine off were restyled valve rocker covers, and all-new secondary reduction and gearbox ratios. These were mainly changed to retain similar overall ratios with the new, higher final drive ratio of 3.09:1 (11/34). This final drive unit itself was the lighter, more compact item of the CX 500, with a heavier sealed U-joint. The overall gearing was slightly lower, improving acceleration, but the general engine and transmission layout was identical to that of the first Gold Wing as described in Chapter Two. All these modifications saw the power rise to 81bhp at 7,500rpm, a figure vindicated by *Cycle* magazine when they managed a standing start quarter mile time of 12.47 seconds at 107.39mph (173kph) from a test GL 1100 in January 1980. The torque was 9.2kg/m at 5,500rpm.

Because the ignition system was now mounted at the rear of the engine the new frame was lengthened slightly. As there was also a requirement for a lower seat height not only was the frame lengthened, but the swingarm was also longer, to provide a

New rocker covers provided immediate visual distinction between the GL 1000 and GL 1100, but there wasa host of internal developments. (Roy Kidney)

massive 1,605mm (63.2in) wheelbase. The new frame featured larger gusseting around the steering head and provided extremely stable steering geometry with a 29.2° steering head angle and 134mm (5.3in) of trail. There were double pinch bolts on the lower triple clamp for greater strength. The frame was also slightly wider to accommodate the larger fuel tank, and lower for a lower seat height. The longer swingarm too came in for some strengthening, the left side now being of square-section rather than pressed steel. Honda's engineers were successful, for the GL 1100's seat height was reduced to 795mm (31.9in) and the motorcycle became significantly roomier than before. It was also more stable, and the disconcerting weave of the GL 1000 K2 and K3 at around 106mph (170kph) disappeared.

Not surprisingly, all-new suspension appeared on the GL 1100. Resisting the trend towards long travel suspension, the Gold Wing development team elected to refine shorter suspension movement with air springing. The fork tube diameter went up to 39mm but inside each fork leg went special low-friction Syntallic bushings constructed of lead, bronze and teflon. These successfully overcame the problem of static friction that had plagued earlier Gold Wings with their all-metal bushings. Although still retaining the usual coil springs, a twin-rate and single-rate stacked on top of each other, most of the support was provided by air pressure. The fork travel was 142mm (5.6in). The two fork legs were linked to a single valve on the top of the right fork tube and, with infinite adjustment between 14 and 21psi provided a significant improvement over the forks of the GL 1000. Air springing too featured on the rear suspension, the twin shock absorbers also having linked air chambers in addition to coil springs and providing 112mm (4.4in) of rear wheel travel. The recommended pressure ranged from 29–42psi and if the shock pressure fell below 28psi a red warning light in the tachometer blinked above a label that cautioned the rider to keep speeds below 50mph (80kph). Compared with other Hondas the Gold Wing suspension was more heavily reliant on air springing because of the sheer mass of the motorcycle. Thus there was proportionately less oil volume in both the forks and shock absorbers: 220cc in each fork leg and 290cc in each shock absorber. As was usual for this era, the FVQ-type shock absorbers didn't provide adjustable damping, but they had four separate damping valves that altered the rebound damping depending on the speed of the stroke.

It wasn't only the frame and suspension that came in for a complete overhaul. The GL 1100 received a new set of Comstar wheels, these having black aluminium spokes with turned-out edges. The front rim width was increased to 2.15in and these now took Dunlop tubeless tyres; a 110/90-19 62H front and 130/90-17 68H on the rear. Rear wheel removal however was not any easier than before, and now required two persons to do this effectively. It meant unbolting the final drive assembly and lowering the shock absorber mounting bolts to tilt the bike on the right side. You just had to hope that the risk of a puncture with the new tubeless tyres was minimal. Completing the upgraded specification were solid twin 276 x 5mm front discs with single-piston brake calipers, and a rear 296 x 7mm disc with a rain shield. While not looking very different, the front brakes were now both fade and pulse-free.

As most Gold Wings ended up with aftermarket fairings (80 per cent according to Honda research), the upright handlebar was designed with a fairing in mind. They were huge, being 843mm (33.2in) wide and extending far back. They also came with steel weights in the end caps to protect the bars and levers in the event of the bike falling over, as well as quelling any vibration. Finally, the trademark dummy 'fuel tank' doors of the GL 1000 were discarded, with all serviceable components accessible through a two-piece lid in the top. It may not have been such a unique solution as before but this was really more practical as the smaller lower lid could now be raised independently to allow for fuel filling without disturbing a tank bag. Inside the larger lid were the fuse box (including auxiliary circuit) and tool kit, although the other electrical components attached to the frame required removal of the plastic 'tank' shell. There was also less storage room than before but the slimmer shape was aesthetically more

pleasing. The redesigned dummy tank also saw the loss of the three gauges that had featured on the GL 1000 K3. Always a hindrance for tank bag placement, the fuel and temperature gauges were now on the top of the instrument panel, with the voltmeter disappearing altogether. This was also the first year of the 85mph limited speedometer.

Further improvement in the comfort level came from the new large two-step luxurious seat, this being adjustable by 40mm fore and aft. The earlier seat had been one item often replaced by an aftermarket product, as was the front mudguard, this now being a more deeply valanced type almost reminiscent of 1930s Indians. What the new mudguard successfully achieved was to keep more road dirt off the bike and rider. Perhaps the most surprising aspect of the completely revised Gold Wing was that it was also lighter than its predecessor, with a dry weight of 266kg (586lb), although this rose to a considerable 288kg (636lb) fully wet. Much of the weight reduction came through the use of plastic for the mudguards, side panels, imitation fuel tank, airbox, and seat base. Also, the exhaust system no longer featured the rust-prone balance box in front of the rear wheel.

Other changes saw a welcome increase in fuel tank capacity (to 20 litres), and a three-phase 300-watt alternator. There was also an additional power point for accessories up to 60-watts (five amps) and the gross vehicle weight rating (GVWR) increased to a good, if still not outstanding, 502kg (1,105lb). This meant that a road-equipped Gold Wing still only had a carrying capacity of 211kg (465lb). The result of this considerable development saw a machine that was an improvement over its predecessor in every respect. The Candy Muse Red, or black, GL 1100 again elevated the Gold Wing to the top of the touring class. This was evident when *Cycle World* ran the GL

1100 up against five other touring motorcycles in May 1980. After being soundly beaten only a year earlier, the GL 1100 was now the class leader ahead of the BMW R100RT, Harley-Davidson FLT-80, Kawasaki KZ 1000, Suzuki GS 850, and Yamaha XS 1100. Honda's development team had been successful yet again.

The GL 1100 Interstate

The GL 1100 that *Cycle World* used in their test was actually the new GL 1100I Interstate. Although the aftermarket accessory business had been supplying full touring equipment for the Gold Wing for five years, Honda in Japan finally realised the potential profit in providing official touring accessories. After consultation with the Gold Wing Road Riders Association, Honda finally produced in the GL 1100I Interstate (GL 1100DX or De Luxe in Europe) the Gold Wing that many touring riders believed they should have made in the first place. Despite some British press scepticism, acceptance of the Interstate wasn't only confined to the United States. The Gold Wing already had attained a cult status in Europe and with the De Luxe Honda expanded the Gold Wing's appeal. Developed in Japan, the Interstate was to be the definitive luxury-touring motorcycle offering the highest quality accessories available. Because they were also factory installed, and specifically designed for a single model, they provided the Interstate with an integrated look that aftermarket accessories often lacked. With this model, Honda effectively killed the aftermarket fairing and luggage industry for Gold Wings, and as the Interstate

It was inevitable that Honda would finally fit a factory fairing and saddlebags to the Gold Wing, these first appearing on the GL 1100 Interstate for 1980. (*Cycle World*)

(and later Aspencade) was so successful in the showrooms the basic stripped Gold Wing also disappeared within a few years.

Since Gold Wing Interstates were factory assembled they came standard with a fairing, rack and rear bag, saddlebags, and engine and saddlebag guards. In Britain, the detachable trunk and saddlebags were extra cost options. All the body pieces were injection moulded plastic, colour-matched to the rest of the motorcycle (in the same colours as the 1980 GL 1100). There were no fairing brackets on the frame downtubes, the fairing mounting solidly and unobtrusively without ugly hose

clamps. It also came with built-in air scoops and adjustable vents. Assembled from two separately moulded inner and outer sections, the fairing provided two pockets, one being lockable. The left pocket had provision for an optional radio/stereo/intercom sound system, including speakers. Also optional was an additional gauge console in the fairing. This could mount four extra instruments, and Honda provided a voltmeter, air temperature, altimeter and a clock. The transistorised Clarion radio was designed and built by Honda, specifically for application on a motorcycle and was full of features including signal-seeking tuning.

The Interstate was an immediate success and continued for 1981 with only small changes. Most noticeable was the lower seat that could also be moved fore and aft. (*Cycle*)

In every respect the Interstate equipment was of the highest quality. Scratch-resistant Lexan was used for the screen rather than the more usual Plexiglass, and the windshield height could be altered 25mm. An even taller optional screen was also available. Although not detachable, the saddlebags (providing 36 litres of storage space) contained a lightweight travel bag, and the rear bag was removable. This also incorporated a passenger backrest. There were locks for just about everything, these totalling 12 for all the various components. The integration of the package was completed with the incorporation of the turn signals in the leading edges of the fairing and lower rear portion of the saddlebags. Practical features continued to a from-the-saddle headlight adjuster and there were large chromed engine bars on either side, these unfortunately being a little too large as they became known as shin-busters.

Despite the GL 1100 having a higher GVWR than earlier Gold Wings, this was now stretched to the limit with the Interstate. All the extra equipment saw the weight of the Interstate rise to 305kg (672.5lb), with the

New for the 1982 Interstate were 18 and 16-inch wheels but the touring capability was retained. (*Cycle World*)

carrying capacity reduced to 196kg (432.5lb). Honda even went as far as to install a 2.5kg (5.5lb) weight between the fork tubes to compensate for the weight lost from the steering axis by the headlight when it was moved to the frame-mounted fairing. Although it wasn't a cheap motorcycle, the Interstate looked like a factory version of most of the customised Gold Wings on American highways and was immediately successful. It was so popular that Honda had plans to cease production of the regular unfaired version but protests from the major American fairing

manufacturers saw the regular GL continue in production until 1984.

For 1981, the GL 1100 received a new seat, this being subtly recontoured and lowered. It was now also possible to slide the seat fore and aft about 40mm using a finger-controlled latch. There was now a higher maximum pressure for the rear shock absorbers (to 57psi; 4kg/m) to improve the ride when fully loaded. The instruments were redesigned with a tinted shield to cover the warning lights, and with improved night time illumination. Other changes saw the adjustable windshield

The Silver Wing

One of Honda's more successful models since 1978 had been the 500cc CX 500, affectionately known by many as 'the plastic maggot'. Not exactly a motorcycle to thrill the senses, there were fewer more sensible machines around than the shaft-drive 496cc V-twin. The CX 500 also came from the same automotive environment as the Gold Wing, being liquid-cooled with crankcase-integral cylinders. Unlike many other motorcycle designs, the 80° V-twin also had chrome-plated cylinders and four valves per cylinder, these being operated by a high camshaft and short pushrods. Very oversquare engine dimensions of 78 x 52mm permitted a 9,700rpm redline. While the camshaft drive was by Hy-Vo chain, unlike the Gold Wing the CX 500 featured a straight-cut gear primary drive to the multi-plate clutch and five-speed gearbox. The shaft final drive used the same 3.09:1 ratio as the GL 1100 Gold Wing.

The gradual development of the CX 500 saw it become the GL 500 for 1981. While the engine layout was ostensibly as before, there was a new chassis, still retaining the engine as a stressed member, but with a single shock absorber Pro-Link rear suspension system. The rear suspension system may have been inspired by the factory racing Hondas but little else, for the Silver Wing was notably heavy and underpowered. As one of the new GL 500 Silver Wings was to be a fully equipped Interstate, the engine was slightly uprated over that of the CX

500. Two Keihin 34mm CV carburettors fed the engine, these being closer together and further back than those of the CX 500 to provide more mid-range power. Completing the up-to-date specification was electronic ignition, and a 252-watt alternator.

The engine was also mounted lower than on the CX 500, and with a wheelbase of 1,495mm (58.9in) the Silver Wing provided full size amenities, but without full size power. The wheels were Comstar, a 2.15 x 19-inch on the front and a 2.50 x 16-inch on the rear, with fat tyres. The rear 130/90 tyre was the same width as that of the much larger and more powerful Gold Wing. There was a single front disc with a dual-piston caliper, and a drum on the rear. A unique feature of the Silver Wing was the modular seat/rear trunk design that could be configured three ways. This was either a dual seat with no trunk, solo seat with a small trunk, and a solo seat with large trunk and backrest. However, even the basic GL 500 Silver Wing was heavy for its capacity at 196kg (432lb) dry. In addition to the basic GL 500 Silver Wing there was the GL 500I, Silver Wing Interstate. This incorporated the factory-integrated Interstate fairing and saddlebags, along with an extra 240mm front disc. The Interstate weighed in at 226kg (498lb) dry, this extra weight being really too much for the 500cc engine to cope with. When tested by *Cycle* magazine in July 1981, the standing quarter mile time for the GL 500 Interstate was an

Endeavouring to expand the Gold Wing's appeal to a less affluent group of riders was the GL 500 Interstate of 1981. Unfortunately, the Interstate was overweight and underpowered. (*Cycle*)

The Silver Wing Interstate provided one of the most effective fairings available for a middleweight, and was a surprisingly agile handler. (*Cycle*)

unremarkable 15.081 seconds at 83.41mph (134kph). This was undoubtedly the penalty for providing one of the largest and most effective fairings available.

Although offering an overweight and underpowered touring motorcycle at a premium price (nearly $4,000 at the time) it was hardly the recipe for success, the GL 500 Silver Wing and Interstate continued for 1982 largely unchanged. Then for 1983, one of the major shortcomings was addressed when the engine was punched out to 674cc for the GL 650 Silver Wing and Interstate. Unlike the Gold Wing development though, to obtain the larger Silver Wing the engine was both bored (to 82.5mm) and stroked (to 63mm). Along with new crankcases, almost every engine component was upgraded, from strengthened big-ends and main bearings, to the clutch and gearbox. There were larger valves (32mm intake and 27mm exhaust) with the carburettor size increased to 35mm.

Chassis developments included the replacement of the Comstar wheels with a normal cast-aluminium type, and a stronger frame. The air-assisted forks had 37mm fork tubes (up from a spindly 35mm) and the damping rates for both the fork and single shock absorber increased. Retaining the modular rear seat arrangement, the GL 650 was undoubtedly an improvement over the anaemic 500, but was still too heavy for a middleweight at 217kg (478lb). Performance though was better than the earlier version, and *Cycle* magazine, in August 1982 managed a fairly respectable standing quarter mile time of 12.96 seconds at 99.55mph (160kph). The Interstate was even heavier at 240kg (529lb). Unfortunately, all this development was still not enough to save the model, and the GL 650 Silver Wing only lasted the one season. While the Gold Wing had shown all the requirements for success, replicating this with a smaller engine wasn't a formula that the touring crowd took to.

Some of the problems of the GL 500 were addressed with the GL 650 of 1983 but the Silver Wing was never a success. (*Cycle*)

constructed of a scratch-resistant polycarbonate. This was the last year before the introduction of self-cancelling turn signals which saw them beep at over 40mph (64kph), and 'click' below that speed as a reminder to switch them off. New colours for 1981 included Cosmo Black Metallic (replacing black), all models featuring orange and gold pinstriping.

For 1982, the basic GL 1100 continued alongside the Interstate, with most changes to the wheels, brakes and tyres. The wheel diameter was reduced, the front going to 18 inches and the rear to 16 inches, although for this year, the black reverse Comstar wheels were retained. The rim width increased to 2.50 inches on the front and 3.00 inches on the rear. These wider rims allowed for larger section tyres; a 120/80H18 F11 on the front and a 140/90H16 K127 on the rear, the rear Dunlop Qualifier tyre being designed to provide increased mileage. Rear tyre life was always a criticism of the Gold Wing, and was now increased to around 15,000 miles (24,000km). This was an important consideration given the difficulty that came with removing the rear wheel. To accommodate the larger rear tyre the swingarm was also slightly wider. The wider section tyres also saw the gross vehicle weight rating increase slightly, by 11.4kg (25lb). Accompanying the smaller diameter wheels were revised third, fourth, and fifth gears, these being slightly higher. There were also new final drive gears, with a different ratio and wider and coarser ring and pinion teeth for additional strength. The ratio of 3.100:1 was similar to before but the teeth were 10/31 instead of 11/43. From the CB 900 came new slotted front discs, with twin-piston floating brake calipers.

Other changes included self-cancelling indicators, the first time these had been fitted since the prototype of 1974. This was a remarkable sophisticated system controlled by a small computer mounted under the steering stem. Sensing steering head turning of as little as 2°, the computer measured the bike's speed and computed the distance travelled. At more than 23mph (37kph) the indicators would self-cancel after five seconds, and below that speed they would cancel after 120 metres (130yd). The five-amp accessory point was uprated to 10 amps and the generator output increased at low and mid-range engine speeds (from 8.2 amps to 11.6 amps). Further engine developments saw changes to the gearshift cam, this now turning in ball bearings rather than the engine cases, and a 2mm larger spark advance shaft bearing. More stringent EPA requirements saw the ignition timing advance slightly slower than earlier Gold Wings.

In response to complaints from owners, the 1982 Interstate received shorter engine protection bars, these no longer banging the rider's shins. The Interstate saddlebag lids too were more water tight and there were new air-cushion passenger footrests. All Gold Wings now had two helmet locks. There were also new colours for 1982, with the GL 1100 and Interstate being available in black and Candy Wineberry Red in addition to the previous Cosmo Black Metallic.

The GL 1100 Aspencade

Almost as significant as the release of the Interstate in 1980 was the introduction of a new super luxury version, the GL 1100 Aspencade for 1982. With the Aspencade, Honda redefined the definition of comfort and conveniences in a production motorcycle, moving into another realm. With a name inspired by the Gold Wing rally at Aspen,

The first really luxurious Gold Wing was the GL 1100 Aspencade of 1982. This came standard with an AM/FM stereo radio cassette and an on-board air compressor. This is the 1983 version. (*Cycle World*)

Colorado, so luxurious was the Aspencade that even the Interstate looked poorly equipped. The basic engine and running gear of the Aspencade were identical to that of other 1982 Gold Wings, but while all these received twin-piston brake calipers, the Aspencade had vented, cast stainless steel disc rotors front and rear, similar to those on the CBX 1000. Yet it was the features that set the Aspencade apart. Central to these was the signal-seeking Clarion Type II AM/FM stereo radio, programmable for stations, with a remote handlebar station selector, a muting switch, a digital dashboard readout, and a clock. If this wasn't enough there was also the option of an auto-reverse cassette tape deck, a 40-channel CB transceiver with handlebar channel selector and talk switch, and an intercom system. The number of locks rose to 14 and in terms of motorcycle equipment there was just nothing else like it in 1982.

Another production motorcycle first was an on-bike air compressor that could adjust the air-assisted suspension simply by pressing a button in the console on the dummy tank top. The small electric compressor itself fitted inside the top of the dummy tank and drew its air through a reservoir incorporating a filter and dehumidifier. Thus the air going to the shock absorbers was cleaner and drier than from other pump systems. The pump only operated when the ignition switch was in the 'P' or 'park' position but it only took five seconds to completely inflate an empty rear suspension system after bleeding. The revised air suspension for the Aspencade also allowed for a slightly reduced seat height over the standard Gold Wing of 780mm. There were other features specific to the Aspencade that were not shared with the Interstate. The passenger backrest was larger, with two storage pouches accessible even while moving. The rear trunk even included a vanity mirror, along with a map

case. Also, in providing a high quality toolkit, the Aspencade Honda had every convenience covered. Rear wheel removal was easier on the Aspencade than on earlier models as the rear guard was removable and the licence plate holder hinged. Many features of the Aspencade, such as the new Type II stereo, 40-channel CB transceiver, and on-board air compressor were also offered as an option for the Interstate. Setting the Aspencade apart were classy, specific two-tone colours, this being either Sterling Silver Metallic/Tempest Grey Metallic, or Sorrel Brown Metallic/Harvest Gold Metallic. The performance of the Aspencade too was only slightly below that of the Interstate, and *Cycle* magazine, in August 1982, still managed a respectable standing start quarter mile time of 13.51 seconds at 97.29mph (157.5kph). The only real down side to the Aspencade was yet another increase in weight, to 319kg (702.3lb) dry, this rising to a massive 348kg (766lb) fully wet. Weight apart though, the Aspencade was still a remarkably easy machine to manoeuvre, and despite limited ground clearance was a surprisingly stable handling motorcycle. Again, the basic excellence of the Gold Wing layout was vindicated but the emphasis was still undeniably that of straight line cruising. In this environment it was unequalled.

Honda didn't let up with the development of the Gold Wing for 1983. Just as Yamaha and Kawasaki started to make inroads into Gold Wing territory, Honda seemingly upped the ante four notches. As before, there were three versions of the GL 1100 available, all sharing the same basic engine and chassis developments. Inside the engine were further alterations to the gearing, with a slightly lower first gear (to 2.64:1) and a higher secondary reduction. This higher secondary reduction raised the overall gearing by about 8 per cent but top gear acceleration was now sluggish

below 60mph (100kph) even though fuel economy and engine life were improved. Considering that Honda had lowered the gearing of the first GL 1100 in 1980 to overcome criticism of the lack of top gear acceleration, this seemed a retrograde step. It was also doubtful if Honda really needed to improve the engine life of the almost unburstable Gold Wing.

Most of the changes were to the brakes, wheels and suspension, the unified braking system (UBS) being the most significant. With refined ventilated disc brake rotors, the hand brake lever controlled the left front disc while the brake pedal activated both the rear brake and right front disc through a pressure control valve. Most of the time the front to rear braking ratio remained constant, until the advent of an emergency when the forward weight transfer saw a proportioning valve reduce power to the rear brake. Honda's TRAC (torque reactive anti-dive control) was unlike other hydraulic anti-dive systems in that it used front brake torque reaction to provide an anti-dive force. However, as the two front discs operated independently, there was a TRAC on each fork leg, offering four positions of adjustment.

In addition to the TRAC, the 39mm forks received some upgrades. The third stage of fork springing was stiffened by 10 per cent, and the compression damping increased by 7 per cent to reduce the risk of the forks bottoming out. The rear shock absorbers were also modified, with more reliance on coil springs than air. The spring rate was 50 per cent stiffer than before and the shock could now be run without any air pressure if desired. Apparently, high air pressures increased seal pressure against the shock's shaft, increasing static friction. With this reduced reliance on air springing the low-pressure warning light disappeared. Other chassis developments saw a VF 750S V45 Sabre-style alloy fork brace and

New opposition

Given the success and following that the Gold Wing enjoyed, it didn't surprise anyone that Yamaha would endeavour to counteract it at some stage. What was probably surprising was the time it took for the XZV12TK Venture to appear, two versions being released for 1983. Yamaha chose a totally different engine layout to Honda, the Venture being powered by a compact liquid-cooled 70° V-four. In many respects it was also a more modern design than the Gold Wing, with double overhead camshafts, four valves per cylinder, downdraft 34mm Mikuni carburettors, counterbalancer and a fully electronic ignition and ignition advance. A bore and stroke of 76 x 66mm gave 1,198cc and 90hp.

The chassis too was more advanced than that of the Gold Wing, with 40mm air-assisted forks featuring anti-dive valving, and a single rising rate linkage rear suspension. The braking system too was integrated, the rear brake pedal also activating the right front disc through a proportioning valve. Realising that the American market demanded full equipment, the Venture offered similar features to that of the Gold Wing Interstate, with an integrated fairing and saddlebags along with a removable trunk. On paper, the Venture certainly looked to have the Gold Wing beaten. The engine provided more power, enough to hustle the 304kg (670lb) Venture through the standing start quarter mile in 12.69 seconds at 103.92mph

(167kph) as tested by *Cycle* magazine in June 1983. Also, the Venture was undoubtedly more competent on twisting roads than the Gold Wing. With the Venture Royale the features too were comparable to those of the Aspencade, the Royale coming with automatic suspension levelling, a full sound system and two-tone paintwork. The sound system too was more sophisticated than the Type-II Gold Wing's, automatically raising the volume to compensate for engine and wind noise at highway speeds.

Also released for 1983 was Kawasaki's attempt to muscle in on Gold Wing territory, the ZN1300-A1 Voyager. Although based on the liquid-cooled 1,300cc double overhead camshaft in-line six that had been around since 1979, the Voyager was completely outfitted with full touring equipment. With a dry weight of 381kg (829lb) and a gigantic 1,645mm (5ft 5in) wheelbase, the sheer size of the Voyager almost made the Gold Wing look small. While producing an impressive 117hp and offering full equipment including a trip computer, the expensive (a list price of $8,299 in the USA) ZN1300 Voyager never really threatened the supremacy of the Gold Wing. Although it lasted through until 1988, in 1986 Kawasaki released their four cylinder ZG1200 Voyager XII, this being a more effective alternative to the Gold Wing but still somehow not managing to emulate it.

Eight years after the first Gold Wing Yamaha released their full-dress tourer, the 1,200cc Venture. The Venture was a very advanced machine and the Gold Wing's first real competition. Here are the 1983 Venture Royale and Gold Wing Aspencade. (*Cycle World*)

11-spoke cast-aluminium wheels. Evidently, market research indicated a customer preference for alloy wheels over the Comstar, although Honda still maintained the Comstar was just as strong. Both the passenger's and rider's footpegs were flatter, the passenger's now being adjustable fore and aft, with slight up and down latitude, and the seat height lowered to the 780mm of the 1982 Aspencade. All Gold Wings received a removable section of the rear mudguard for easier wheel access. The self-cancelling turn signal system was upgraded to that of the V45 Sabre. Some problems with the earlier fork-steering sensor saw the installation of additional speed and distance sensors. Now, if the handlebar sensor wasn't triggered after five seconds, the computer scanned the bike's speed. The determining speed for cancellation was increased to 28mph (45kph) but at slower speeds the distance remained at 120 metres. A final convenience improvement was the installation of a thumb-operated lever-type choke instead of the earlier push-pull control. Changes to the instrumentation saw an end to the annoying 85mph speedometer, this now reading a somewhat optimistic 150mph. Also, as was usual, there were slightly different colours, the black GL 1100 being joined by Candy Regal Brown.

On the Interstate and Aspencade there was yet another change to the engine protection bars, these flaring outwards to provide more legroom. There were also some changes to the seat and rear trunk to improve passenger comfort. The seat was lengthened 30mm (1.2in) between the front and rear humps, and the rider's bucket narrowed by 30mm to provide less passenger leg splay. In response to complaints that the passenger backrest was too low, the entire trunk was relocated 30mm further backwards and 25mm higher.

The Interstate's backrest was also enlarged, all ensuring that the passenger now had little to complain about.

While the top-of-the-line Aspencade was undoubtedly the most highly equipped touring motorcycle available in 1982, Honda went to some effort to ensure this continued in 1983. By far the most striking update was an all-new liquid-crystal instrument display panel. With motorcyclists a notoriously conservative lot this was a daring development, and one that would ultimately fail to be widely accepted. However, there was no doubt that the LC display provided some exceptional features for the day. Electronic readouts informed the rider of both the road and engine speeds, along with fuel level, engine temperature, suspension pressures and trip distances. As a trip computer it also calculated the remaining distance if the trip mileage was pre-entered. The tachometer readout could be switched between a digital display or graph and there was also a green service light that turned yellow at 8,000 miles (1,300km) and red at 9,000 miles (1,450km). There was now no excuse for not having your Gold Wing serviced at the correct time. The only mechanical element in the instrument panel was the odometer. The Gold Wing had always been packed with features, and the 1983 Aspencade raised these to a new level.

Although the same on-board air-suspension compressor from the 1982 model was retained, there were changes to the plumbing and the display incorporated in the liquid-crystal display panel. As long as the bike wasn't moving, suspension pressures could be adjusted even with the engine running and with the ignition switched 'on' rather than 'park'. The pressure control buttons were now located on the fork crown and pressing

Raising the level of equipment on the 1983 Aspencade was this liquid-crystal instrument display panel. As well as incorporating a trip computer just about every aspect of the engine's condition could be determined. (Roy Kidney)

the selector button switched the digital engine bar graph into a suspension air pressure graph. This was tricky stuff for 1983. Aspencade colours for 1983 too were new, with Nimbus Grey Metallic/Achilles Black Metallic and Candy Wineberry Red/Bramble Red Metallic introduced.

All these developments saw the Gold Wing, particularly the Aspencade, continue to be one of the leading touring motorcycles. With annual average sales of around 25,000 the Gold Wing remained the most popular touring motorcycle in America, but the competition from Yamaha's new Venture was undeniable. In July 1983, *Motorcyclist* magazine picked the Venture as the best big tourer so it was inevitable that Honda would retaliate. The result was the all-new GL 1200.

Although the flat-four cylinder engine layout was retained, almost every engine component was new on the GL 1200. (Roy Kidney)

Further expansion: 1,200cc

Although denied by Honda engineers, there was no doubt that Yamaha's Venture, and the impending Harley-Davidson Electra Glide Classic with the new Evolution engine, had Honda worried. This prompted the design of a completely new Gold Wing for 1984. The resulting GL 1200 was not only an enormous improvement over the GL 1100, it was also intentionally designed to maintain a classic link with earlier Gold Wings. While it did not look much different externally to the GL 1100, there was little that was shared between the two models.

Shuji Tanaka headed the design team, this being his final year as GL project leader, and he was reported to be extremely pleased with the resulting GL 1200. The difficulty came in providing a motorcycle that offered more, but didn't interfere with the touring culture that now surrounded the Gold Wing. Honda could easily have discarded the flat-four engine layout in favour of a V-four. They were already heavily committed to that engine layout, and there were even rumours of a V-six and an opposed-six. However, market research indicated that owners still wanted a flat-four, and any new arrangement would have been seen as insulting to the legions of GL owners. Also, the flat-four layout was undeniably more suited to a large touring machine than a V-four. The

benefits that were apparent back in 1975, such as a low centre of gravity for easy handling in such a large machine, were even more evident as the weight of the Gold Wing increased.

Superficially the GL 1200 engine looked to be a development of that of the GL 1100, itself derived from the first GL 1000. Yet while the basic engine and gearbox configuration, along with the cylinder bore centres were unchanged, almost every component was new. Only the water and oil pumps were the same, and they were driven at different speeds. With the Yamaha Venture being more powerful than the GL 1100, it was inevitable that there would be a displacement increase, this growing to 1,182cc with yet another bore and stroke change (75.5 x 66mm). The bigger bore brought more flat-topped pistons, and a slightly lower, 9.0:1, compression ratio. The redesigned cylinder heads also provided more squish area. In order to increase intake velocity the inlet valve diameter was reduced 2mm, to 36mm, but the exhaust valves remained at 32mm. The 1200 also received new camshafts, not only providing 9mm of valve lift (on both inlet and exhaust), but also more overlap and duration. A major, and welcome, development to the valve train was the addition of Honda's maintenance-free hydraulic valve actuation system. This used an eccentric rocker shaft to

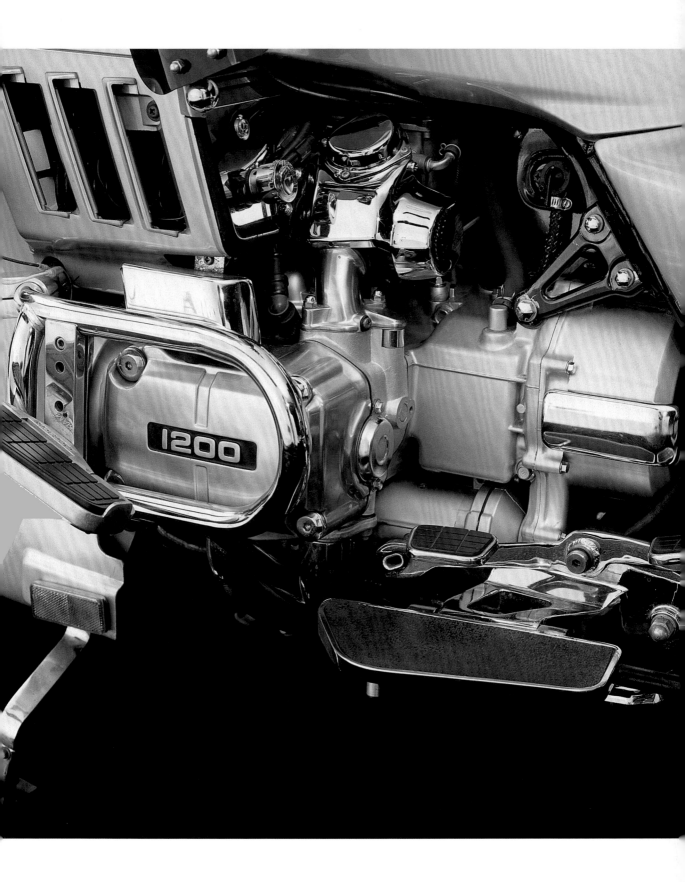

New for the GL 1200 were hydraulic valve lifters, these eliminating another maintenance chore. (*Cycle*)

maintain the correct valve clearance, the system resembling that used in many cars. A hydraulic lifter, pressurised with engine oil, bore on a flat machined into the rocker shaft and a spring-loaded plunger acted in the opposite direction on another flat. As the camshaft spun and actuated the rocker arm, the eccentric shaft rotated, raising or lowering the rocker arm to maintain the correct valve clearance. To save further weight these adjusters and rockers

fitted in a magnesium rocker cover. As before the camshaft drive was by 17mm toothed rubber belts, but these were now 88-tooth (still with trapezoidal teeth). Unlike the belts on the GL 1100, these belts were also now interchangeable with some models of Honda car.

Already strengthened considerably when it made the transition from 999cc to 1,085cc, the only lower end modification was an increase in

The counter-rotating alternator was now oil cooled, but would be problematic. The carburettors were again 32mm. (*Cycle*)

the main crankshaft journal diameter, to 52mm, the crank now spinning on high performance Kelmet bearings. There were some clutch modifications. Clutch actuation was now hydraulic, eliminating another maintenance task, and the clutch had an additional plate. The earlier coil-type clutch spring became a diaphragm type. Although retaining the Gold Wing trademark counter-rotating alternator, this was now oil-cooled and the output increased to 360-watts. It also incorporated a new drive system to reduce low-speed noise and vibration. There was now a centrifugal drive mechanism that engaged a clutch-like spring damper above 3,000rpm. Below that speed diaphragm springs locked the system, this being disengaged by ball and ramp

arrangement at higher engine speeds. A smaller and lighter two-row radiator also replaced the previous three-row unit, flowing more air than before, and including an electric fan. Also electric, rather than mechanical, was the fuel pump. Although the developmental emphasis was clearly on simplifying maintenance, the GL continued with the awkward canister-type oil filter. Considering other Hondas were moving towards the use of the spin-on cartridge style this seemed a strange oversight.

After switching around with the carburettor sizes on the GL 1100, there was a return to Keihin 32mm constant vacuum carburettors with the GL 1200. Still fed by a plenum chamber on top of the engine, with a cylindrical

paper air filter element, the carburettors were tilted to smooth incoming air. A development with the aluminium bodied (rather than zinc) carburettors was the use of thin, more responsive, Hydrin diaphragms. The air cleaner volume was also increased and there was a freer breathing exhaust primary chamber. To optimise power and economy there was also a revised electronic ignition system, this incorporating a vacuum sensor to advance the ignition timing up to a further 13° when the engine was in fourth or fifth gear. Cutting out the vacuum advance in the lower three gears eliminated the vacuum-advance-induced surging that had characterised some earlier engines. While the internal ratios were unchanged, the GL 1200 had much taller overall gearing, largely due to a 12/34 (2.83:1) final drive ratio. This meant that fifth gear was effectively an overdrive, with an overall ratio of 3.62:1.

As expected, the GL 1200 engine was also increased in size slightly over that of the GL 1100. Although the same length (601mm), it was 32mm wider (697mm) and 5mm taller (487mm), without carburettors. The power went up to 94hp at 7,000rpm, with a 13 per cent increase in torque to 10.7kg/m (75.2ft/lb) at 5,000rpm. What was particularly improved was the torque at low revs. At only 2,500rpm the torque was 9.3kg/m (65.3ft/lb), providing vastly improved top-gear roll on performance over the 1983 GL 1100 despite the higher gearing.

While the engine was all-new, the chassis too was cleverly modified to provide an impression of lightness and nimbleness belying the considerable weight of the fully outfitted touring GL 1200. Thus not only was there a new double-cradle steel frame, with the engine being moved forward, but there was upgraded suspension, and perhaps the most significant alteration, smaller diameter wheels. Both the front and rear wheels were downsized from

those of the GL 1100, to a 16-inch front and 15-inch rear. The rim sizes remained at 2.50 inches on the front and 3.00 inches on the rear but the sizes of the tyres increased to a Dunlop Qualifier F11 130/90-16 and a K627 150/90-15. Not only did the smaller front wheel provide a quicker steering response, but chassis changes saw a substantial difference in the overall geometry. The steering head was moved down 30mm and back, and the engine moved forward 63mm and canted 3° upwards. Additionally, the swingarm pivot was moved forward and also lowered 30mm, with the length increasing 56mm. The swingarm pivoted on taper roller bearings and was constructed of 58mm box-section steel tubing (instead of 50.8mm) with wider legs to accommodate the larger rear tyre. All this contributed to more weight on the front wheel and improved mass centralisation, meaning better handling, and improved legroom. The steering rake was also increased slightly, to 30°, although the trail was decreased slightly to 118mm.

Handling was also improved through a stronger front fork, the tube diameter increasing to 41mm. There were stiffer fork springs, and the compression damping reduced by 20 per cent. Adjustable damping still wasn't a feature, but the TRAC anti-dive system was retained, although this was now on both fork legs. While many Hondas were going towards a single shock absorber Pro-Link rear suspension system, the requirement for under-the-seat fuel tank space saw the GL 1200 retain the dual shock system. Along with stiffer springs the shock absorber rebound damping increased by 46 per cent. As with the previous GL 1100, both the forks and shock absorber springing was air-assisted. Fork travel was increased slightly, to 140mm, and the rear wheel travel up an inch, to 105mm. The braking was the same unified system as before, with the Aspencade receiving vented discs, 276mm

The final year for the basic unfaired Gold Wing was in 1984 when it had a round headlight in a chrome shell and a free standing taillight assembly. (Author's collection)

on the front and 296mm on the rear. The brake pads were sintered metal.

The result of these developments was the GL 1200 steered and handled like a much smaller bike. To achieve this with a machine with a wheelbase of 1,610mm (63.4in) and a wet weight of nearly 360kg (790lb) was a considerable engineering feat. The GL 1200 provided light handling even from walking-pace-like speeds, and the steering and handling maintained composure even through corners, something that could rarely be said about earlier Gold Wings. There was even more ground clearance due to the more forward and tilted placement of the engine, with an increase in the banking angle by 2°.

Of course, comfort wasn't forgotten with the design of the GL 1200. The shape of the huge

stepped saddle was similar, but with firmer foam than before. In usual Gold Wing fashion the seat was adjustable fore and aft, the release lever now being located inside the dummy tank rather than under the seat. The final year for the basic unfaired GL was 1984, this being available in black or Candy Wineberry Red. So well designed and functional was the factory-fitted fairing and luggage of the Interstate and Aspencade that buyers just tended to go straight for one of those, overlooking the considerably cheaper unfaired version. The fairing was even more effective on the GL 1200 Interstate and Aspencade than before. Honda employed a wind tunnel to design the fairing and the luggage, as a complete aerodynamic package to reduce buffeting and noise. Still air behind

There was a revised Aspencade for 1984, with a wind tunnel designed fairing. US versions like this received fairing-mounted mirrors.(*Cycle World*)

the fairing was increased through the attachment of side wings, these also deflecting the main air stream off the rider's arms and shoulders. The fairing-mounted mirrors too were designed to deflect air from the rider's hands, although UK versions featured handlebar-mounted mirrors. As before, the windshield was adjustable, although this was still a relatively time-consuming task.

All-new luggage was included in the Interstate and Aspencade specifications, with the rear trunk now no longer removable. The top of the trunk was also extended upwards for more passenger back support. Luggage volume in the trunk increased by almost 50 per cent, and it could now easily accommodate two full-face crash helmets. There was a further 15 per cent increase in the capacity of each of the side bags, and because they were fixed there were lift-out liners. Accompanying this was an improved luggage sealing system, with a more precisely manufactured tongue-in-groove rubber seal, this being incorporated in the luggage bodies rather than the lids. The bag's lids were also easier to remove and replace, this being one of the criticisms of the earlier luggage system. Each fairing pocket offered 21 litres of storage, even on the Aspencade as the radio was now located in the centre of the fairing above the handlebar. With an additional 2.7 litres in the top of the 'tank', the GL 1200 Interstate and Aspencade were well endowed with carrying capacity. The Interstate was available in three colours for 1984: Candy Wineberry Red, Pearl Siren Blue, and Senior Grey Metallic.

The top-of-the-range Gold Wing continued to be the Aspencade for 1984, with the usual increase in equipment over its cheaper brothers. Central to this was a new-generation Hondaline Type III radio system, built by Panasonic. Much lighter and more compact than the earlier Type II, it featured a signal-

A new digital display appeared for the 1984 Aspencade, without the earlier bar-graph tachometer. (*Cycle World*)

seeking AM/FM radio with a digital display and four programmable buttons, along with an auto-reverse tape deck, intercom, and manual and automatic muting. An expensive option on the Interstate, there was also a handlebar-mounted remote control for radio station tuning while on the move, and an automatic volume control that compensated for road speed. These handlebar controls made for a massive cluster of switches on the left side, although much more simplified than on earlier Aspencades. An optional set of headsets was available, as was a CB radio and intercom. The radio may have had poor night-time illumination, but the sound was at least as good as most cars and the features were even better than most.

While the regular GL 1200 and Interstate retained their dual analogue instruments, the Aspencade received a slightly revised digital

system. The bar-graph tachometer from the 1983 Aspencade went in favour of a digital readout only. To warn of the impending 7,500rpm limit a red horizontal light flashed from 6,500rpm, remaining on above 7,500rpm. LCD read outs continued for the speedometer, trip mileage, gear position, fuel gauge, air suspension pressure and coolant temperature. The only analogue readout was the odometer, while the fuel gauge remained as pessimistic as before. The temperature gauge doubled as that of the suspension air pressure, and was still filled by an on-board air compressor. Now operable only with the ignition switch on, a sensor in the speedometer determined only that the bike was not moving. The compressor and controls were now located in the lower right section of the fairing and included a useful air outlet and hose to inflate tyres or an air mattress, if required.

Gold Wing rallies

Central to the Gold Wing culture is the rally. Bringing together thousands of enthusiasts, these are a total celebration of the Gold Wing and have become an annual pilgrimage for Wing Nuts everywhere. All the major Gold Wing associations hold rallies, the largest being the Wing Ding, the official annual rally of the Gold Wing Road Riders Association. Operating since 1978, the 23rd event was held at Greenville, South Carolina on 3–6 July 2001. The Wing Ding is much more than a rally and get-together for motorcyclists sharing an interest in the Gold Wing. Here, over four days, Gold Wing owners can see the huge range of aftermarket products and accessories available, and indulge in a well-organised range of activities. These extend from poker runs to technical seminars regarding the ownership and maintenance of a Gold Wing. If there is too much on offer there are so many magnificently presented Gold Wings to observe that cameras can be kept busy for hours.

The Gold Wing Touring Association also organises national rallies; during 2001 these were the Gold Rush at Ozarks Osage Beach Missouri, and Camp Wing Tyme at Moses Lake Washington. The American Gold Wing Association annual National Rally is the 'Gold Classic' for 2001 being held at Goreham, New Hampshire, on 18–21 June 2001. Wing Dings are also held in England, although on a considerably smaller scale than in America, the Wing Ding on the Isle of Wight in 1999 for example attracting 350 Gold Wings. In Europe annual rallies, also known as Treffens, with each European owners' club organising their own international Treffen. Gold Wing owners, more so than any other single model owners, have embraced the annual rally with alacrity. So much so that the rally has become integral to the culture of ownership and brings Gold Wing owners together into an almost religious brotherhood.

Gold Wings are all about riding and the open road beckons for the Gold Wing as it does for no other motorcycle. One of the essential destinations is a Gold Wing rally. (*Australian Motorcycle News*)

The new range leader for 1985 was the expensive, and opulent, GL 1200 Limited Edition. (*Cycle World*)

New for the Aspencade for 1984 were passenger footboards and elbow rests, and an 'Aspencade' signature light across the rear of the trunk. The trunk incorporated a map and document case along with a vanity mirror. Other special luxury touches included a special tool set in an embossed pouch. There was also a wide range of options, including a digital voltmeter, chrome front mudguard trim, guard rails for the trunk and saddlebags, a top trunk luggage rack, and exhaust extensions. Another improvement with the GL 1200 was the increased load capacity, to 172kg (380lb). Three colour options were available for the Aspencade for 1984, these being Pearl Saturn Red/Century Brown Metallic, Premium Beige Metallic/Grace Brown Metallic, and Pearl Siren Blue/Achilles Black Metallic.

So how did the GL 1200 shape up compared to the increased opposition? Honda engineers certainly managed to cleverly disguise the weight, but the engine still wasn't quite as strong as that of the Venture. *Cycle* magazine, testing an Aspencade in February 1984, managed a standing start quarter mile in 13.34 seconds at 89.54mph (144kph). Undoubtedly the flat-four engine layout was better suited to a touring motorcycle and the GL 1200 was far less top heavy than the Yamaha, and much better balanced than the six-cylinder Kawasaki Voyager. It seemed to be agreed that the GL 1200 was a vast improvement over the 1100, but still not hugely superior to the Yamaha Venture. Still, the GL 1200 was just what Honda needed to maintain their position as the sales leader in large touring motorcycles. The Venture may have been close, but the GL remained the standard by which all touring motorcycles were judged.

After five years as project leader, Hideaki Nebu replaced Shuji Tanaka as head of the Gold Wing design team. Tanaka had presided over the most significant developments in the

history of the Gold Wing and remained a member of the team. After ten years the basic unfaired Gold Wing became a thing of the past. When the Gold Wing was conceived the concept of factory-supplied fairings for both touring and sports bikes was almost unheard of but the success of the Interstate and Aspencade with their factory-fitted fairings and luggage was unprecedented. By 1985 it was unprofitable to produce the plain base Gold Wing, the market demanding ever more-featured touring motorcycles. Thus the Interstate became the base model, and an even higher specification Limited Edition took over from the Aspencade as the range leader.

As the GL 1200 of 1984 was an all-new design, there were only detail changes to the Interstate and Aspencade for 1985. New ducting in the fairing provided improved air circulation in the rider's still-air bubble, and a push-to-cancel turn signal sat up on the left handlebar, also providing a longer cycle (seven seconds instead of the earlier 5.5 seconds). One area where the Gold Wing was constantly being changed was the internal gearing. Touring riders never seemed totally happy with the gearing and 1985 saw changes to first, now 36/14 (2.57:1) and fifth, 28/35 (0.80:1). While the primary, second, third, fourth, and final drive ratios remained unchanged, the secondary drive (linking the transmission output shaft to the driveshaft) was lowered to 36/37 (0.973:1). The intention of these gearing changes was to improve acceleration, and Honda's design team certainly succeeded. The engine speed at 60mph (100kph) increased slightly from 2,096rpm to 2,977, but the GL 1200 was almost sprightly compared to the 1984 model. Testing an Interstate in January 1985, *Cycle* magazine managed a standing-start quarter mile time of 12.73 seconds at 103.76mph (167kph). Still available in three colours, the 1985 GL 1200 Interstate came in

Starshine Silver Metallic and Telstar Blue Metallic in addition to the usual Wineberry Red. Also basically unchanged for 1985 was the Aspencade, but as always new colours distinguished the model. These were still two-tone: Pearl Vintage Red/Mahogany Red Metallic; Satellite Blue Metallic/Spiral Blue Metallic; and Sandy Beige Metallic/Grace Brown Metallic.

The GL 1200L Limited Edition

Designed to commemorate Honda's 25 years in America and the Gold Wing's tenth anniversary was the GL 1200L Gold Wing Limited Edition. If the Aspencade had previously set the standard for luxury motorcycling, with the GL 1200L, Honda raised expectations even higher. This was the model that stated the Gold Wing was now well and truly an American motorcycle. It wasn't so much that all GL 1200Ls were produced in Marysville, Ohio, it was more the fact that the Limited Edition epitomised American-style touring. Loaded with gizmos and gadgets the 1200L wasn't only luxurious; it was expensive, at a listed $10,000. This placed it nearly $4,000 more than the Interstate and more than $2,000 over an Aspencade. So what did the buyer get for this considerable price tag? Basically, every accessory ever considered for a motorcycle, and then some. The American consumer loved gimmicks and gadgets and the GL 1200L delivered.

It was difficult to believe that the already highly specified and opulent Aspencade could be enhanced, but the Limited Edition almost made the Aspencade appear a stripped model. The basic engine was shared with the

Aspencade, but due to popular demand computerised fuel injection (CFI) replaced the bank of Keihin carburettors. This wasn't designed to improve engine performance, but rather to improve throttle response, cold starting, and fuel economy. Using sensors to monitor throttle position, engine speed, manifold pressure, air pressure and air and engine temperature, the CFI not only provided the correct mixture but also adjusted the ignition curve. Unfortunately, while the computerised fuel injection was good in theory, in practice the injected bikes did not seem to run as well as the normal carburetted versions. The gearing was the same as other 1985 GL 1200s but the 1200L came with a much more powerful (490-watt) alternator to power its barrage of accessories.

And these accessories were plentiful. Using an actuator powered by the engine's vacuum was an electronic cruise control. This operated the throttle drum via a control cable linked in series with the throttle-grip cables. The cruise control worked only in fourth or fifth gear, between 30 and 80mph (50–130kph) with the actuating switches on the right handlebar. There were 13 fail-safe cut-off mechanisms, including braking, gearshifting, engine speed exceeding 6,800rpm, and manual throttle closing. With micro switches handling set and resume functions, as well as acceleration and deceleration, the cruise control feature was a welcome addition for long trips. Just like the Aspencade, the GL 1200L also featured an on-board air compressor, but with an additional function. Auto-levelling rear suspension (ALRS)

A rider would never be bored on the Limited Edition, with the Electronic Travel Computer providing a bewildering array of functions. (*Cycle World*)

The Limited Edition's specification included running lights in the saddlebags. (*Cycle World*)

was included to maintain the preset factory ride height to compensate for loads. A touch of the switch on the left handlebar activated the shock preload adjusting system. In addition to the cruise control and adjustable suspension, the 1200L came with a trip computer and two additional rear speakers for the Panasonic Type III audio/intercom system. These were mounted on top of the plush armrests and there was a tank-mounted 'joystick' sound balance control. The electronic travel computer sat in the forward portion of the dummy fuel tank and provided the rider with hours of entertainment. This included fuel consumption (instantaneous and average), the amount of fuel used and remaining, cruising range, trip mileage, elapsed time, and average trip speed. There was even a small map of the United States to locate different time zones to adjust the clock automatically. Whether the trip computer was actually a necessity was debatable, but it certainly set the 1200L apart.

Completing the GL 1200L's upgraded specification were running lights on the saddlebags and fairing, and cornering lights illuminating the area beside the bike when the turn signals were activated. The rear trunk now had an interior light. All this extra equipment saw an inevitable weight penalty, with the wet weight of the Limited Edition rising to 375kg (826lb). Even so, the GL 1200L was only a little less brisk than the Interstate on the road and at

the dragstrip. *Cycle* magazine, in February 1985, achieved a standing start quarter mile in 12.88 seconds at 102.32mph (165kph). Available for one year only, the GL 1200L Limited Edition was also only produced in one set of colours; Sunflash Gold Metallic with Valiant Brown Metallic inserts.

If many had been sceptical that Honda could market and sell a $10,000 motorcycle they were proved wrong when the GL 1200L Limited Edition became spectacularly successful. Those buyers seeking exclusivity may have been disappointed, but the Limited Edition proved so popular (and profitable) that it was inevitable that another series would appear for 1986. This year the model gained the title GL 1200SE-i, or Aspencade SE-i, and a new colour scheme of Pearl Splendour Ivory with Camel Beige Metallic. Fortunately for those owners of

The Sunflash Gold GL 1200L Limited Edition was only
available for 1985 and represented the pinnacle of full-
dress touring for those that could afford the hefty price.
(*Cycle World*)

the earlier Limited Edition, their special
Sunflash Gold colour scheme would at least
remain unique to that model.

There were also three GL 1200s for 1986, the
Interstate and Aspencade in addition to the
SE-i. There was an effort to even further reduce
engine vibration and all engines received
hydraulic tappets with a slightly larger oil
capacity to reduce valve-train noise. Revised
valve timing boosted the mid-range power and
the redesigned transmission gears also
featured smaller engagement slots for the gear
dogs to reduce driveline lash, always a small
problem with the Gold Wing. Other changes
were limited to the addition of a splash guard
on the rear mudguard. The Interstate featured a

trunk-mounted taillight and stoplight assembly
and there were fewer colour options this year,
with black joining the Wineberry Red. As the
middle-of-the-range model, the Aspencade
also came with the new splash guard, as well
as upgrades to the Type III radio with the
addition of Dolby noise reduction. There were
some slight colour variations, Twilight Beige
Metallic with the red; Pearl Marlin Blue with the
Spiral Blue; and Trophy Silver Metallic with
Tempest Grey Metallic.

All the features of the GL 1200L Limited
Edition were offered on the Aspencade SE-i, in
particular the computerised fuel injection. The
pursuit of less exhaust emissions saw a
recalibration of the computerised fuel injection,

More opposition

Just as Honda was unveiling their new GL 1200, one of the original inspirations for the Gold Wing was undergoing a significant update. Harley-Davidson's Electra Glide Classic had been soldiering on for many years with only small updates, and even in 1984 was still powered by the cast-iron 'shovelhead' engine. It may have had electronic ignition, but in terms of sophistication the Electra Glide was a long way removed from the Gold Wing. Then, for 1985, the Electra Glide was transformed with the installation of the new five-speed 1,340cc Evolution engine. No longer did the engine overheat or leak oil, and for the first time, the Electra Glide could be seen as a realistic alternative to the Gold Wing. However, it all came too late. By 1985 the Gold Wing was entrenched as the premier long-distance motorcycle while the Electra Glide offered a supplementary option, not a replacement. With the release of the GL 1500 in 1988 the Electra Glide was again seen as down on power, wind protection and carrying capacity.

A more serious threat to the supremacy of the Gold Wing came from the other Japanese manufacturers. Given the expansion of the full-dress shaft-drive touring market from 1980 it was no surprise to see Suzuki mount a challenge. With their GV 1400 Cavalcade of 1985, Suzuki provided a full list of features, which on paper, more than matched the Gold Wing's. Like Yamaha, Suzuki also went for a liquid-cooled V-four double overhead camshaft engine, the Suzuki unit being an 82° V-four displacing a massive 1,360cc. The engine had four valves per cylinder and was fed by four 33mm Mikuni carburettors. Rolling on 16-inch wheels front and rear the Cavalcade was available in two

forms, the full specified LX being even larger and heavier than the Gold Wing Limited Edition. The wheelbase was a long 1,675mm (65.9in) and the LX tipped the scales at 342kg (754lb) dry, 8kg more than the 1200L. Only Kawasaki's massive Z1300 Voyager weighed more.

The top-of-the-line Cavalcade LX seemingly offered more than enough to cause the more expensive Honda GL 1200L Limited Edition some worry. Features included cruise control, an automatic volume control stereo, on-board self-levelling suspension, and even an air cushion seat. Yet there wasn't really enough to put the Cavalcade above the Gold Wing and Venture and it struggled in the marketplace. For 1987 there was an even more luxurious Cavalcade LXE, but by 1990 the Cavalcade was dead, a victim of the excellence of the new six-cylinder GL 1500.

After three years, Yamaha too had found it difficult breaking into Gold Wing territory, so for 1986 they enlarged the Venture to 1,294cc (79 x 66mm). Developments saw electrically activated anti-dive, and the suspension controlled by a computer levelling system. This still wasn't enough to displace the Gold Wing and in 1994, after ten years' production, the Venture too disappeared. The year 1986 also saw Kawasaki re-enter the fray with their in-line four-cylinder ZG 1200 Voyager XII. The huge Z1300 Voyager had never proved especially popular and the engine design was ageing. In many respects the new Voyager provided the most competition for the Gold Wing. The in-line four-cylinder engine was a Kawasaki trademark and the Voyager XII had an all-new double overhead camshaft, liquid-cooled, four-valve 1,196cc (78 x 62.6mm) engine with hydraulic valve adjusters. Much of the chassis mimicked the Gold Wing, including 16 and 15-inch wheels, full fairing with sound system, air-assisted suspension, and a Gold Wing-style dummy fuel tank. The dimensions were fairly standard, with 1,620mm (63.7in) wheelbase and a dry weight of 317kg (699lb). While the Cavalcade and Venture were eventually crushed by the GL 1500, amazingly the somewhat underdeveloped Kawasaki Voyager XII resisted, and it built its own niche market. The Voyager XII remains in production, and while it hasn't earned a following to rival the Gold Wing, there is a national owners' club in the USA, the American Voyager Association.

For 1985 Suzuki too endeavoured to encroach on the Gold Wing market with their highly specified Cavalcade LX. Powered by a 1,400cc V-four engine it was even larger and heavier than the Gold Wing Limited Edition. (*Cycle World*)

Replacing the Limited Edition for 1986 was the Aspencade SE-i. This would be the final fuel injected Gold Wing until the new GL 1800 for 2001. (*Cycle World*)

this now being less efficient than before as the engine suffered hesitation when cold. There was also the same auto-levelling rear suspension system, but on the SE-i the predetermined rear end setting was stiffer to firm up the ride. The Type III stereo now included Dolby noise reduction and of course there was the trip computer, cruise control, additional running lights, and cornering lights. Weighing in at a slightly higher 384kg (847lb) wet, the engine developments for 1986 didn't make the SE-i perform any more strongly than the earlier Limited Edition. *Cycle* magazine, in January 1986, managed to hustle their SE-i through the standing start quarter mile in 12.91 seconds at

101.62mph (163.5kph). However, the fuel injection stumble, and the susceptibility of the trip computer to water-induced failure saw the end of the highly specified SE-i after 1986.

The final model year for the flat-four engine was 1987 and there were now only two models in the Gold Wing range, the Interstate and Aspencade. Repositioned at the head, the Aspencade now incorporated some of the features of the earlier SE-i, including cruise control and Type III sound system with handlebar controls. The fairing was redesigned slightly to cover the oil filter cover and accept auxiliary driving lights, and there was a revised ventilation system. Other features now standard included

The GL 1200 still commands a loyal following, especially amongst those who believe the flat-four engine was the classic Gold Wing layout. This Aspencade is as well presented as many later Gold Wings. (Roy Kidney)

passenger floorboards and armrests, the trunk mirror and ventilated brake discs. All Gold Wings now featured a revised drivetrain, said to reduce noise by 10 per cent. The driveshaft bevel gears were now helical, rather than straight-cut, and there were revisions to the damper spring and cam, as well as the clutch plates and gearshift mechanism. The result was a noticeable improvement in quietness and gear selection.

Another area that came in for refinement in the final year of the GL 1200 was a new tapered seat with three-stage foam. After many years Honda had finally got the seat right and the new shape was wider for both passenger and rider, with an undercut backrest separating them. The new colours for the 1987 Interstate were Pearly Beige Metallic or Amethyst Grey Metallic, and there were three colour variations for the Aspencade. Candy Wineberry Red/Dusky Red Metallic; Black/Tempest Grey; and Pleiades Silver Metallic/Spiral Blue Metallic. The additional equipment also saw an increase in the dry weight of the Aspencade to 337kg (743lb).

So, after 13 years, the traditional flat-four Gold Wing engine finally came to an end. It had not only earned itself an enviable reputation for reliability, but was also one of the most charismatic Japanese engines ever. Sales had exceeded 270,000 and the Gold Wing had been so successful that as time wore on there was a deepening conservatism regarding the GL's development. It seemed that the greater the legend, the greater the reluctance to tamper with it. Because the flat-four engine lasted so long and so many examples were manufactured there is now a resurgence in interest in those final GL 1200s. They are now considered the last 'real' Gold Wings in some quarters, and the drivetrain developments meant that the 1987 GL 1200 in particular was an especially well-developed touring motorcycle. The final GL 1200 was the end of an era, but a new age was about to begin.

For 1990, the highly specified SE version joined the GL 1500. Distinguished by its Pearl White, the SE also featured a built-in windscreen vent. (Roy Kidney)

Six cylinders

No matter how great the legend, Honda was inevitably forced to replace the venerable four-cylinder Gold Wing. The passage of time, and the encroachment of competitors into the Gold Wing market, required a new design. The flat-four engine had also reached the peak of its development with the GL 1200, but Honda was predictably cautious when the creation of a replacement began during 1983. They began by canvassing loyal Gold Wing supporters to give them the direction they should take. Wingers want more of everything. More power, more smoothness, more features and more luxury. The new Gold Wing needed to extend the parameters of American-style touring and become the definitive two-wheeled luxury platform.

More engine meant more cylinders, and here the inspiration came from the first M1 prototype of 1973. Considering that the M1 project leader had been Soichiro Irimajiri, and he was now the head of American Honda, it wasn't that surprising to see the flat-six engine resurface. While that engine had been deemed too long for installation in a motorcycle chassis, time had moved on, as had the increase in overall acceptable motorcycle dimensions. With a wet weight of 400kg (883lb) and a giant 1,699mm (66.9in) wheelbase, the large, powerful and roomy new-generation GL 1500 Gold Wing made the 220kg (484lb) M1 seem anorexic. In developing the Gold Wing replacement over a four-year period, Honda built 15 different machines in 60 prototype stages, including 20 separate engines. Thousands of hours were

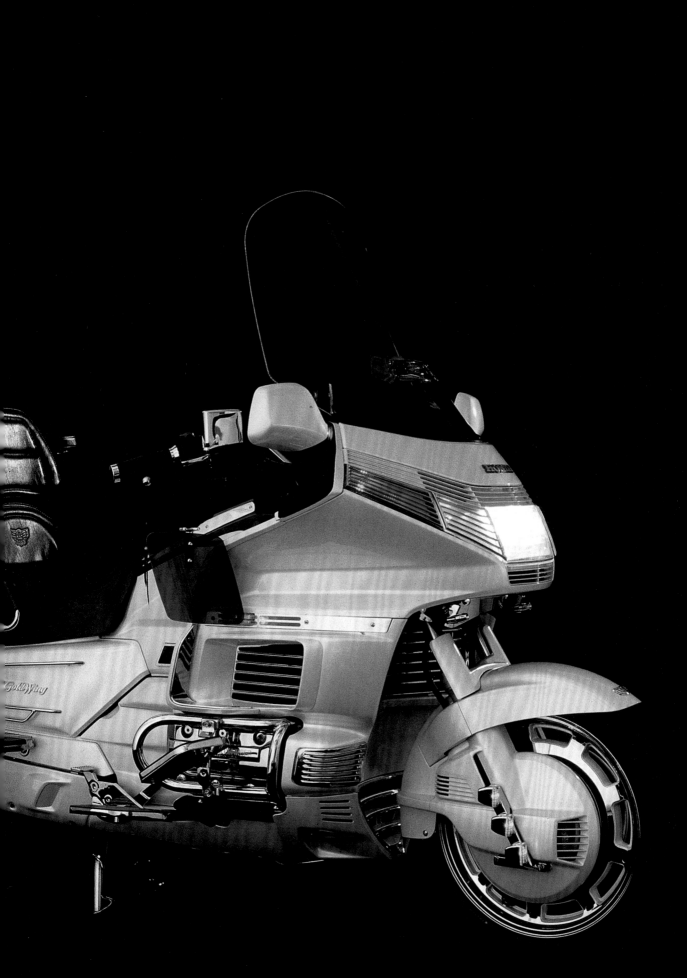

The heart of the GL 1500 was a new 1,520cc six-cylinder engine that was even smoother, and provided more power and torque than the earlier 1,200cc four. This is a 1989 model with 'GL 1500/6' engravings on the rocker covers. (Roy Kidney)

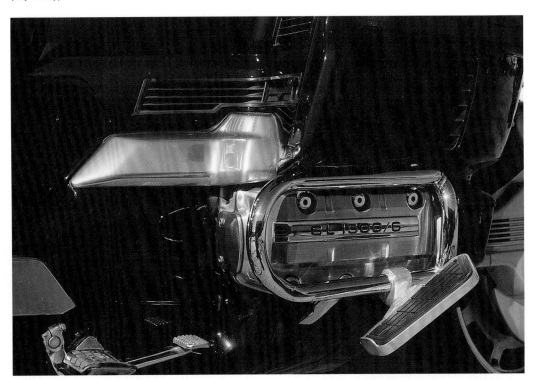

spent testing and engines were routinely run near redline for the equivalent of 60,000 miles (100,000km). This was the most comprehensive model development project in Honda's history. So important was the new Gold Wing to Honda that it had to be right.

No longer derived from the first GL 1000, the GL 1500 engine was completely new, while retaining many of the earlier four's features. With dimensions of 71 x 64mm, the total displacement was 1,520cc, and as each individual cylinder was smaller than that of the 1200 four, the GL 1500 engine was even smoother than its predecessor. While both the flat-four and flat-six layouts provided perfect primary and secondary balance, the crankshaft layout for the six allowed for 60° crankpin spacing rather than 90°. The original GL 1000 had been designed initially as a high performance engine (it had an 11,000rpm

redline and provided Superbike performance) and had been softened gradually over the years, but the GL 1500 was envisaged as a touring engine from the outset. There was no need for double overhead camshafts, four-valves per cylinder, or multiple carburettors. High revs were never a consideration, and the redline of 5,500rpm was 2,000rpm lower than that of the GL 1200. Thus the single overhead camshaft, two-valves per cylinder layout was retained, the two camshafts still being driven by toothed rubber belts. However, the 17mm belts were new, being 87-tooth as with the GL 1000 and 1100, but not being interchangeable as the teeth were now semi-circular. There was no doubt that with the GL 1500 the emphasis was on smoothness, quietness, and refinement. Torque, not power, was the aim.

There was more of an automotive influence in the design of the GL 1500 than the earlier four. Whereas the four had exhibited a number of motorcycle design features, notably in the clutch and transmission, the new six drew heavily on Honda's automotive division. Gone was the Hy-Vo primary drive chain, the primary drive now being by 78/49 (1.59:1) helical gears at the rear of the crankshaft. The drive was still through a motorcycle-type wet multi-plate clutch (now counter-rotating because of the gears), and the gearbox shafts were still mounted underneath the crankshaft and cylinder heads for a lower centre of gravity. The gearbox featured cluster gears integral with the mainshaft, with the shifting forks mounted on a sliding dog. This design had already been a long-term feature on Honda cars. Not only were the number of parts (sliding gears, bearings, and shims) reduced, but the benefits were also a reduction in noise and mass. After years of notchy gearshifts, the GL 1500 shifted better than any earlier Gold Wings, but there was still room for improvement. The gearbox didn't invite aggressive shifting, and if shifted too fast it could be jerky and noisy. The ratios too for the five-speed gearbox were all new, but the most significant addition was an electric reverse gear operated by the starter motor for easier low-speed manoeuvrability. Here was another Gold Wing first. It involved a pair of planetary gears, one for starting and one for reverse, plus an idler gear connecting the starter to the final drive gear. An interlock mechanism held the gearbox in neutral while reverse was engaged. Pulling a hand lever on the left side deployed the interlock and the reverse gear engaged the final drive gear through an idler at a 660:1 reduction ratio. Keeping the starter button down saw the Gold Wing reverse at about 1mph (1.6kph). Several lockout mechanisms protected the reverse system. It could only be operated with the engine running, the gearbox in neutral, and the sidestand retracted. Transistors shut the

system down if the engine stalled, and there was a speed limiter and bank angle sensor that cut the power if the bike tipped too far. Honda had thought of everything with this device.

Quietness was also a high priority, and helical gears also drove the fifth gear overdrive, the 34/35-tooth (0.97:1) secondary drive, the 34/12 (2.83:1) final drive, and the Gold Wing-trademark counter-rotating alternator. The only chain now was a Hy-Vo spinning the oil pump. Not only was noise reduction a major concern. New for the GL 1500 was a revised system of hydraulic valve adjusters, these no longer using the complex rotating eccentric rocker shaft system of before. The GL 1500's rocker arms pivoted on a fixed shaft, one end bearing against the cam, with the other directly on the valve stem. To close the lash each valve rocker meshed with an eccentric spindle moving in step with an automotive-type lifter situated in the upper cam box.

Other low-maintenance features included a spin-on oil filter (finally), an idle adjuster positioned next to the tank filler cap, and a new air-cooled alternator. Now providing 546 watts (up 60 per cent over the GL 1200), this was not only considerably more powerful but as it sat outboard of the engine cases it was easily accessible. The earlier oil-cooled alternator required removal of the entire engine to replace in the event of failure, a common occurrence if overloaded with electrical accessories. The resulting six-cylinder engine was a tribute to excellent design, being only 63.5mm longer than the four, and weighing 118kg, up 10kg.

Following the lack of acceptance of the earlier computerised fuel injection system, it was no surprise to see the GL 1500 rely on carburettors to feed the six cylinders. However, these carburettors were complemented by a sophisticated electronic engine management system. Fuel injection would also have boosted the price, but so complicated was the induction

system that fuel injection may have been a simpler solution. Using only two 36mm Keihin downdraft diaphragm-type carburettors bolted to a high, six-tube manifold, these were controlled electronically to provide accurate fuel metering under all conditions. With a maze of wires, hoses and black boxes, it looked dauntingly complex, and certainly didn't encourage owner investigation or repair. There were eight sub-systems monitoring air and engine temperature, manifold pressure, altitude, rpm, and gear position to manage the intake and ignition. It was almost like having electronic fuel injection with carburettors and the GL 1500 moved into another dimension of complication.

Central to the induction system was a liquid-heated intake manifold. As the GL 1500 engine operated in a strictly controlled narrow operating range, the high rise inlet manifolds tended to run too cool. Thus engine coolant was routed through the inlet manifold to stabilise intake temperature. Temperature was also regulated in what Honda called the 'Hot Air Intake System'. Here, a bimetallic valve drew warm air from the exhaust system up into the airbox if required. A 'Primary Main Jet Air Control System' regulated the airflow. This system consisted of three primary jets, one main and two secondary jets operated by computer-controlled solenoids. Sensors to the computer monitored intake manifold pressure, air intake pressure, and rpm, triggering the solenoids to open or close the jets for optimum air intake. There was an additional 'High Altitude Compensation' system, a bellows-type regulator triggered by a barometric sensor increasing airflow above 3,000ft for leaner running.

Computers abounded, and there were further processors for the usual electronic cruise control and the ignition. The digital ignition monitored manifold pressure, air temperature,

engine speed and coolant temperature to provide two different advance curves. These were tied to the gearbox, one for first and second gears, and one for the top three gears. There was also a further computer system plugged into the intake manifold. With their emphasis on maximum low-end power the camshaft timing was exceptionally mild, with zero valve overlap. However, zero overlap valve timing, while effective at boosting bottom-end power, also caused the pressure to build inside the combustion chamber and intake manifold during deceleration with the throttle closed. In exceptional circumstances this could cause a disconcerting rear wheel hop.

Honda could have used a one-way clutch arrangement to counter this rear wheel lock up, but for the GL 1500 their cure was the even more complicated 'Air Shot System'. Here, air was drawn from the airbox into the intake manifold to decrease vacuum, and consequently engine braking, when required. Impulse generators in the inlet tracts regulated this controlled vacuum leak. There was no shortage of sensors and California models received even more valves and hoses for their evaporative emissions control. Even the fuel pump was temperature sensitive, decreasing flow for leaner running at high temperatures. This was now located inside the fuel tank to ensure quietness and prevent vapour locks in the fuel line. The fuel tank was still located underneath the seat, but was slightly larger at 23.8 litres.

The cooling system consisted of two radiators, mounted in a 15° vee behind the front wheel, and with a compression ratio of 9.8:1 the claimed maximum power was 95hp at 5,000rpm. However, it was tractability Honda was after with the GL 1500 and the engine pulled cleanly from as low as 700rpm until the redline. With the maximum torque of 15.3kg/m produced at only 4,000rpm, the GL 1500 could loaf around in 'overdrive' top gear with plenty of power available without downshifting. The entire engine and drivetrain system may have been complicated, but there was no denying that, in spite of some gearshift clunkiness, it worked admirably. Also, the sheer capacity of the GL 1500 ensured that even the dragstrip performance was more than acceptable. *Cycle* magazine, in March 1988 managed a respectable standing start quarter mile in 13.24 seconds at 97.23mph (156kph). Not bad for a motorcycle designed way outside the dragstrip environment.

It wasn't only the engine that was new for the GL 1500. The computer-designed frame moved away from the earlier tubular steel type and was undoubtedly influenced by the newer generation sports bike frames such as that of the VFR 750. Consisting of two huge rectangular 35 x 80mm box section steel main load-bearing members running straight from the steering head to the swingarm pivot, there was a tubular steel engine cradle and rear section. The downtubes were removable to allow easier engine servicing, the engine also being rubber mounted to further reduce vibration. The engine was positioned as close as possible to the front wheel for optimum mass centralisation while a bolt-on rear subframe supported the saddlebags. The swingarm too, with the shaft housing on the right and rectangular beam on the left, was stronger than before. The steering geometry also encouraged stability, with a rake of 30°, with 113mm (4.4in) of trail.

To further improve high speed stability, the previous 16-inch front wheel made way for an 18-inch. A 16-inch wheel was used on the rear, and the rims were half an inch wider than before. The front 3.00 x 18-inch wheel mounted a 130/70-H18 Dunlop K177 Touring tyre, and the rear 3.50 x 16-inch wheel had a 160/80-H16 Dunlop K177. The casting of the wheels

showed some concern about reducing unsprung weight with ten short, hollow spokes connecting a hollowed-out hub to the rim. This design was unique to the GL 1500 and still featured on the 2000 Model. Further evidence of weight saving came through bolting the vented dual front 296mm discs directly to the hub. As on the previous Gold Wing, the braking system was unified, the rear brake pedal activating the right front and rear 316mm disc twin-piston calipers, while the handlebar lever operated only the left front disc. The suspension too was really only a development of that of the GL 1200. However, after several years of reliance on air springing, this became less important with the GL 1500. The front 41mm TRAC-equipped fork featured the same Syntallic bushings, but lacked any air adjustment. The vertically mounted rear twin shock absorber suspension only received air assistance on the right shock, while the left shock absorber only featured a non-adjustable coil spring. As before though, the GL 1500 featured an on-board air compressor that allowed for the right shock absorber air pressure to be adjusted at the flick of a switch. To lower the seat height of the GL 1500 over the GL 1200, the rear suspension travel was also reduced, to 85mm (3.3in). The front forks provided 140mm (5.5in) of travel.

With the rear suspension air pressure set around 32–40psi, the inherent advantages of the horizontally opposed cylinder layout and the under-the-seat fuel tank were again evident with the GL 1500. Here was a large touring motorcycle that handled with incredible lightness at walking pace speeds, yet could be hustled through the mountains and fast sweepers without wallowing or grinding the undercarriage excessively. The ground clearance was much improved over earlier Gold Wings, and the handling inspired more confidence.

The new fairing and its integrated headlamp gave the GL
1500 a much more modern look. (Roy Kidney)

The stereo was now located in the dummy tank cover and even the SE now reverted to analogue instruments. (Roy Kidney)

When it came to underpinnings Honda took an almost car-like approach to the Gold Wing. As the next generation Gold Wing it was almost inevitable that the design would evolve even closer to that of a two-wheeled car and the fully enclosed bodywork didn't encourage owner interference. Underneath the bodywork was surely the most complex equipment ever seen on a motorcycle, but it certainly didn't detract from reliability. The downside was when it came to serviceability. The earlier Wings were not known for easy rear wheel access, but with the GL 1500 rear wheel removal almost called for an authorised Honda dealer. The huge disassembly process was illustrated in the owners' manual and required 'mechanical skill and professional tools such as a floor jack'. Hardly the sort of equipment most riders would carry on a trip.

Unlike in previous years, there was no 'stripper' Interstate or Aspencade available, only one variant of the GL 1500 being offered for 1988. As such the level of equipment was predictably lavish. Central to the design was fully enclosed ABS plastic bodywork, designed with careful attention to air management. From the grey plastic brake covers directing cool air into the engine bay, to the smoothly integrated luggage and body panels isolating the rider from engine heat, the GL 1500 moved into a new era. The fairing, with dual headlights shining through a flush-fitting cover, provided the ultimate in weather protection, with the windshield being adjustable up-and-down by 75mm without tools. There were also plenty of vents incorporated in the fairing, including two heater vents to direct warm air on to the feet. Honda even cut small intake ducts in the mirror mounts to slightly pressurise the cockpit and reduce negative pressure waves on the rider's back.

So effective was the riding environment at isolating the elements that it was as automotive as possible on a motorcycle. Colour-matched plastic panels covered every unsightly surface, including the handlebar, and all the switches and controls were designed with style and ergonomics in mind. The digital instrumentation of the GL 1200 Aspencade disappeared, replaced by the more usual (and easier to read) analogue dials. There was a slightly more accurate fuel gauge, and a low-fuel level warning light. Other warning lights were for main beam, sidestand low oil, and an OD to indicate overdrive was selected. The stereo functions were displayed on a digital screen between the speedometer and tachometer, the stereo itself being moved from the dashboard to the dummy tank cover. All the features were there, a 24-watt per channel AM/FM radio, stereo cassette with auto reverse, integrated intercom, and an automatic sound control. There were only two dash-mounted speakers, although the space for optional rear speakers was provided in the trunk lid.

Comfort considerations extended to a deep, well padded seat, this no longer offering fore-and-aft adjustment. However, this was really no longer needed as the riding position was roomier than before. The passenger was even better catered for, with padded back and armrests, and floorboards. The integrated luggage not only provided more storage capacity than the GL 1200 (two litres more in the trunk alone), the single central-locking key operation was easier to operate. Three levers at the base of the trunk operated all three luggage compartments. There was no shortage of factory options available, the list of 28 items ranging from a CB radio to trunk spoilers, running and cornering lights, and colour-matched lower-leg air vents. The colours for 1988 emphasised greys and beige. These were Dynastic Blue Metallic/Pewter Grey Metallic; Phantom Grey Metallic/Checker Black Metallic; and Martini Beige Metallic/Haze Brown Metallic.

The Pacific Coast

As the Gold Wing grew to become an even more specialised big-rig long-hauler, Honda sought to extend their more automotive approach to motorcycles to include a mid-range general purpose machine. This appeared during 1989, in the form of the Pacific Coast, and which was quite different in execution to their earlier attempt at a mid-displacement Gold Wing, the ill-fated Silver Wing. In many ways the Pacific Coast was a mini-GL 1500, and designed to appeal to a new group of buyers, those that probably hadn't previously considered a motorcycle.

With the styling entrusted to Honda's car division, Hondawaco, the Pacific Coast was even more automotive in appearance than the GL 1500. Then, under the direction of the motorcycle styling division, the engine and chassis disappeared under a sea of plastic. Although it was almost impossible to tell, underneath the all-compassing bodywork was a rubber-mounted 800cc (79.5 x 80.6mm) 45° V-twin engine that originally came from the VT 750 Shadow cruiser. First introduced in 1983 the five-speed liquid-cooled engine featured staggered crankpins to provide perfect primary balance, chain-driven single overhead camshafts, and three valves per cylinder. Carburetion was by two Keihin 36mm downdraft CV carburettors. As the engine was difficult to access, maintenance-free features included the sealed battery, hydraulic valve adjusters, automatic camchain tensioners, and a hydraulic clutch. Of course, there was shaft-drive and the frame was similar in design to that of the GL 1500. There were two rectangular steel main spars, the other frame tubes being tubular steel. Also Gold Wing-inspired was the under-the-seat fuel tank, and almost vertically mounted twin rear shock absorbers, although

there was no air-assist. The front forks were similar 41mm with TRAC, and the wheels featured short hollow spokes with the brake rotors bolted directly to a hollowed-out hub.

In other respects though the Pacific Coast differed markedly from the Gold Wing. The front brake calipers came from the CBR 750 and operated independently of the rear brake, this being a rod-actuated single leading shoe drum. The wheel diameters too were smaller, with the Pacific Coast having a 17-inch front and 15-inch rear. Although no lightweight at 262kg (578lb) dry, the Pacific Coast was surprisingly agile, mainly due to the low centre of gravity and low seat height (765mm). The automotive influence in the design of the bodywork took that of the GL 1500 a step further. Not only were all the handlebars and controls hidden away behind plastic covers, but the rear section imitated a car trunk. A lid with a gas-charged shock absorber revealed motorcycle-like saddlebags, although these were really too small to be very useful.

Although not a hugely popular model, the Pacific Coast was deleted from the line-up in 1991, only to make a surprising return for 1994. It lasted until 1998 with only minimal annual alterations, mainly colour changes, and from 1997 the front disc cover was removed. Honda envisaged the Pacific Coast as a lifestyle motorcycle, a 'must have' accompaniment to a range of quality appendages. With its full coverage bodywork the Pacific Coast was undoubtedly ahead of its time, but somehow missed the mark. The Gold Wing may have appealed to a breed of riders outside the mainstream of motorcycling, but like the earlier Silver Wing, the Pacific Coast lacked the charisma and aura of the Wing.

Another spin-off from the Gold Wing was the Pacific Coast of 1989. Taking an automotive approach to the middleweight class, this lasted through until 1998. (*Cycle*)

All 1988 GL 1500s were also characterised by the '1500/6' emblem on the right rear saddlebag. This was to be the final year that Gold Wings were manufactured in Japan.

Not surprisingly, the GL 1500 rewrote the parameters for touring motorcycles, and was hailed as the most significant touring machine since the first Gold Wing of 1975. *Motorcyclist* magazine voted it 1988 Bike of the Year and *Cycle* magazine, in a 1,000-mile-day tour test, found the GL 1500 superior to all competitive Japanese full-dress tourers. For a first year model the GL 1500 was surprisingly trouble free. However, as it was such a complicated design with so many new components there were a few teething problems. Apart from the drivetrain, complaints arose about the windshield adjuster, cruise control, saddlebag seals and fork action. There were also isolated instances of clutch and ignition failure. For the next model year production was to be only in the USA and there were few changes, and these mainly to the colour combinations. While the Martini Beige continued, the familiar Candy Wineberry Red made a return (with Burgundy Red Metallic), along with Commodore Blue Green Metallic/Triton Blue Metallic. Instead of being grey the front brake covers were now colour coordinated on green and beige models, and the rear saddlebag '1500/6' emblem deleted. The GL 1500 also began to make its mark in Europe, although for Germany local market requirements saw a smaller rear trunk and lower screen.

After two years with minimal development, for 1990 there was a host of mechanical improvements to the GL 1500, as well as an additional higher specification model, the SE. All these developments were aimed at silencing the critics, and included doubling the number of shifting dogs on the first through to fourth gears to reduce driveline lash and smooth out the shifting. These gearbox modifications were accompanied by changes to the hydraulic clutch action and an increase in the gearshift lever throw. Both the carburetion and camshaft timing were altered to improve driveability while still meeting emission requirements, and the troublesome cruise control electronic logic was revised. This now allowed speed adjustment in 1–6kph increments. Other changes extended to a windshield screen adjuster that was easier to use and improved sealing for the saddlebags. The rubber strips around the lids were now moulded to follow the contour of the bags' openings. The forks too were reworked for a quieter, smoother action, and increased bottoming resistance, while the rear suspension travel was increased to 104mm (4.1in). New colours accompanied the changes for 1990, the GL 1500 Wineberry Red now having a new secondary colour of Rime Grey Metallic. The only other colours were Carmel Blue Metallic with Snow Shadow Grey Metallic. The front brake cover was coordinated in either red or blue and the general fit and finish of the panels improved in response to criticism.

Following two years as a single model only, it was no surprise to see a higher specification SE (Special Edition) offered for 1990. In the manner of the earlier GL 1200 Limited Edition, the GL 1500 SE came in one colour only: Pearl White with Eagle Silver Metallic and Ocean Grey Metallic accents, along with gold-finished logos. Also setting the SE apart were the two-position passenger footpegs, these being able to be lowered by 60mm for taller passengers. A three-position central vent in the windscreen provided additional cool air, and there were rider-controlled ducts to bring warm air to the feet when required. Other SE features were an improved 25-watt full-logic sound system, illuminated handlebar switches, and cornering lights that came on with the turn signals (as with the earlier Limited Edition). There was an additional rear brake light incorporated in a spoiler mounted on the trunk, and a zippered

Candy Spectra Red, a classic Gold Wing colour, was available on the 1994 SE. The front brake cover was chrome plated from 1991. (Roy Kidney)

pouch at the base of the passenger seat concealed a pullout seat cover. The dry weight of the SE rose marginally to 365kg (804lb).

Celebrating ten years of Gold Wing at the Marysville plant saw three variants of the Gold Wing for 1991, all with commemorative 'Anniversary Edition' badging above the Honda plate on the front of the fairing, and a serial number plate on the dummy tank. This year also saw a return of the 'stripper' Interstate, the previous GL 1500 continuing as the Aspencade, while the SE remained at the top of the range. For a hefty $5,000 less than the SE, the Interstate came without a high-end stereo system, on-board air compressor, cruise control, reverse gear, or saddlebag trunk liners. The Interstate's saddle too was thinner and firmer than the other GL 1500s, also being narrower at the front and providing a slightly lower seat height of 749mm (29.5in). The Interstate's footpegs offered less fore and aft movement for the rider's feet and the passenger no longer had floorboards. Located in the left side of the fairing, rather than on top of the dummy tank, the 10-watt twin speaker Hondaline Kenwood radio was noticeably weak as the road speeds climbed. However, it still offered 10 station presets and a handle-mounted tuning/volume control. While the windscreen was adjustable, the Interstate suffered more from helmet-level buffeting. Apart from the lower seat, where the Interstate really scored over the more lavishly equipped 1500s, there was a reduction of dry weight to 345kg (760.7lb), although this rose to 386kg (851lb) fully wet. Still this was nearly 18kg (40lb) less than the SE and the Interstate provided a slightly sportier and more manoeuvrable feeling. In keeping with the basic nature of the Interstate, only one colour scheme was offered for 1991: Cinnamon Beige Metallic with Valiant Brown Metallic.

As the mid-range model, the 1991 Aspencade provided all the amenities of the 1990 GL 1500, but was only available in black, with special gold emblems, and a chrome front brake cover. Also identical to the previous year was the GL 1500 SE, but the paintwork was the same Sunflash Gold Metallic/Valiant Brown Metallic as the 1985 GL 1200L Limited Edition. There were few changes to the now standard three-model Gold Wing line-up for 1992. The Interstate received a new Panasonic integrated 25-watt AM/FM stereo system with new controls and displays, along with an output jack to plug in a portable cassette or CD player. Other features included a CB radio interface and an intercom. There were also new colours of Candy Spectra Red or Cambridge Blue Metallic. The only changes to the Aspencade and SE were colours; the Aspencade being the same blue and red as the Interstate. The SE came only in a radiant two-tone Teal Blue; Barbados Blue Metallic and Laguna Blue Metallic. However, having obliterated the competition, the Gold Wing was unchallenged as the best tourer available in *Motorcyclist* magazine's 'Best Street Bikes of 1992'. Also for 1992 for the first time were special 'Canadian Edition' versions with emblems on the seat and tank, manually adjustable vented windshields, chrome disc covers, seat cover, and maple leaf key.

After three years without any significant development, there were a few more changes for 1993. On all GL 1500 engines the valve rocker arms now spun on needle roller, rather than plain bearings to reduce valve train friction and noise. There was an upgrade to many of the standard features, particularly on the SE. Now in Pearl Glacier White or Pearl Coronado Blue, in addition to the Teal Blue, standard equipment included the formerly optional 40-channel CB radio and rear speakers. A left handlebar controller now incorporated all the radio functions, and the cruise control was linked to the crankshaft, rather than the speedometer cable, for more precise speed control. Also new were air valves in the front forks for manual adjustment of the fork air

Living with a GL 1200 and a GL 1500

What typified the Gold Wing development year by year was a gradual improvement in comfort and serviceability that by 1983 the huge aftermarket industry was largely devoted to cosmetic accoutrements. This still didn't mean however that the new 1,200cc engine was totally trouble free and there have been numerous stator and charging problems on the GL 1200. If moisture enters the electrical connector between the generator and wiring loom this shorts out, destroying the alternator. As the GL 1200 alternator was oil cooled dirty oil can also affect the generator coating. Main fuses have also been known to crack, causing immediate electrical system failure.

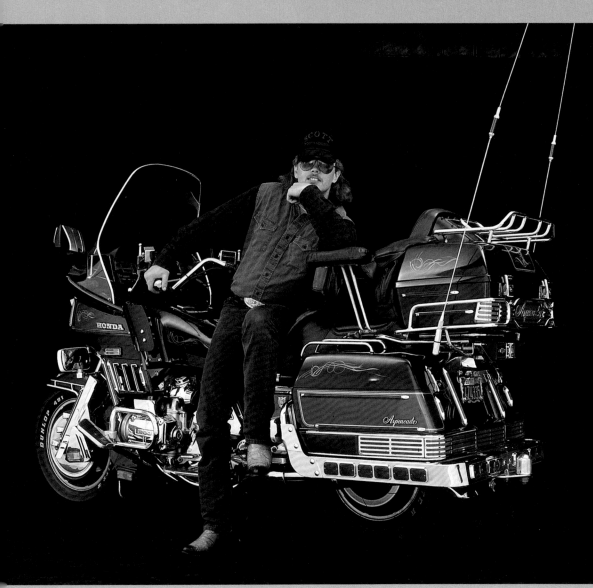

Owners of the GL 1200 are just as enthusiastic, and take as much pride in the presentation of their machines as GL 1500 owners. Even today they are superb touring machines.
(Roy Kidney)

Corrosion can affect frames, centrestand mounts, exhausts, electrical connectors, and rear shock absorber pistons. These wear the seal and allow the air to escape. Replacement shock absorbers and firmer fork springs are the usual modification. If left on the sidestand for protracted periods the fork seals too will fail prematurely. Recommended tyres for the GL 1200 are Dunlop D404, Michelin H-Tour, and Avon Elan. Even nearly 20 years on a GL 1200 is a thoroughly practical, and supremely comfortable, touring motorcycle.

With the GL 1500 came virtually trouble-free running for thousands of miles. Early (until 1992) models could suffer oil leaks from the rocker covers and the clutch was prone to wear. Occasionally the engine could jump out of fourth gear and the

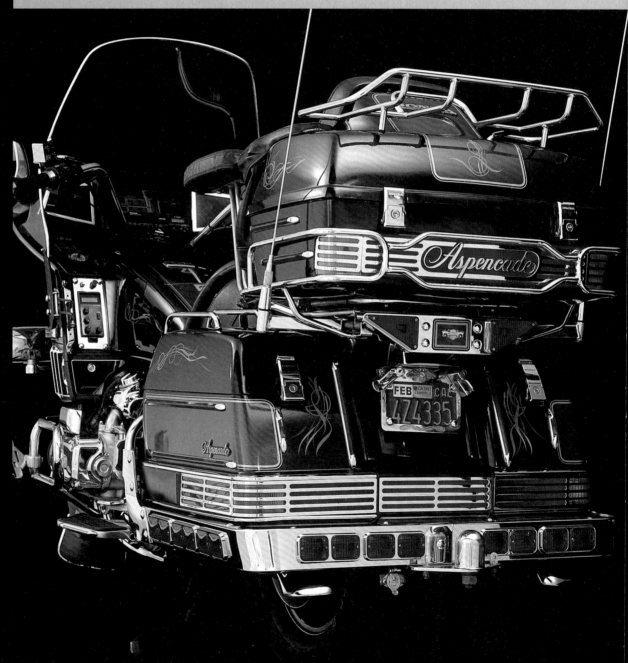

Although now nearly 15 years' old, the range of aftermarket accessories available for the GL 1200 is considerable. (Roy Kidney)

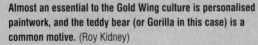

Almost an essential to the Gold Wing culture is personalised paintwork, and the teddy bear (or Gorilla in this case) is a common motive. (Roy Kidney)

alternator still wasn't trouble free. The windings sometimes were not tight enough and could pull on the centre as it spun. Early examples could suffer a failure of the fuel sensor that cut the fuel supply if the bike fell over. This was positioned underneath the right pannier and improved versions have an up-pointing arrow embossed on the side, rather than painted on. There have also been some problems with the operation of the reverse gear caused by poor connections on the two resistors.

High mileage CL 1500s have been known to strip the splines where the drive shaft and final drive meet, but this is really only a problem if the machine is subjected to extreme loads such as pulling a trailer or fitted with a sidecar. The rear drive rubbers were also prone to wear, especially on earlier models (prior to 1992) with smaller rubbers. Moisture can also cause problems with the GL 1500. Exhausts corrode, and the suspension air compressor can fail if the silicon fluid absorbs water. If water enters the weld in the swingarm this can eventually swell and rub on the tyre. In extreme cases it may even break. Other problems

The Gorilla extends beyond the paint to a mascot on the trunk. (Roy Kidney)

are the deterioration of the rear brake line from the inside that results in the outside brake pad jamming on. The fluid doesn't release from the piston and the outside pad (and one side of the disc) will wear prematurely. Also prone to wear are the wheel and steering head bearings. As with earlier Gold Wings, a popular accessory is firmer suspension to improve the handling. This generally includes progressively wound fork springs (from Progressive Suspension), and could also include Magnumatic air shock absorbers. The GL 1500 also suffered noticeable front fork flex that could be improved through the installation of an aluminium fork brace. Recommended tyres for the GL 1500 include Metzeler ME 88 and Dunlop K177 or 491. As

Spectacular attention to detail and wonderful accessories characterise many Gold Wings, yet these machines' main purpose is still to hit the open road. (Roy Kidney)

the GL 1500 has matured the aftermarket has grown to expand on the already impressive list of official Honda accessories, many of these being manufactured in Japan as well as America. One of the areas the aftermarket has moved into is electronic gadgetry, with entertainment being supplied by an interface co-ordinating CD changer, radar detector, and cellular telephone, all with the Honda stereo/cassette player, intercom and CB radio. Achieved through special helmets fitted with headsets, the amusement possibilities were almost endless.

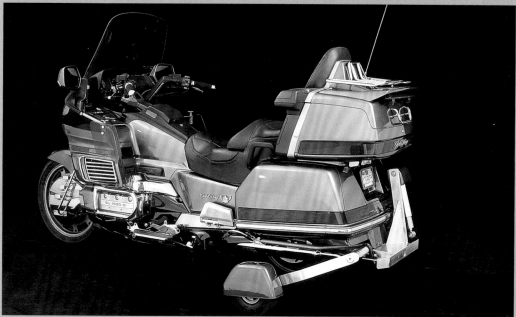

Above: 'Pride & Joy' sums up how this couple feel about their GL 1500. Highlighted on the trunk is 'Destination Friendship', inherent in the Gold Wing culture. (Roy Kidney)

Below: Every conceivable accessory is available for the Gold Wing, and the ultimate in motorcycle stability is surely a set of swivelling outriders. (Roy Kidney)

Throughout the life of the Gold Wing there have been many Limited Edition and Anniversary series and 1995 represented the Gold Wing's 20th anniversary. All 1995 versions received special badges, along with a lower seat and revised suspension. This is the SE. (*Cycle World*)

pressure. The 1993 Aspencade also shared the SE's modified cruise control, as well as receiving the fork air valves. There were no changes to the Interstate apart from colours, the same blue or red being available for both the 1993 Aspencade and Interstate, along with black. It was much the same scenario for 1994, with only colours changing on the three models of Gold Wing. Both the Interstate and Aspencade were Black-Z or Pearl Atlantis Blue in addition to the red, with the 1994 model being delineated by a lower cowling in the same body colour. Colours were

The 20th Anniversary SE also received special trunk and saddlebag liners. All three compartments locked with the ignition key and were well sealed by rubber weather-stripping. (*Cycle World*)

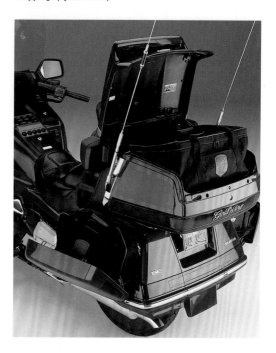

also more standardised for the 1994 SE, with Pearl Bermuda Green joining the previous white, along with the red and blue of the Aspencade and Interstate.

With the Gold Wing's 20th anniversary in 1995, this year was a milestone in the history of the model. While the GL 1500 may not have been directly derived from the 1975 GL 1000, it remained as the standard-setting touring motorcycle. So dominant had the Gold Wing become in that category that of the other Japanese manufacturers, only Kawasaki provided any alternative by 1995. So it was inevitable that there were only small changes to the GL 1500 for the anniversary year. After all, it had been in production since 1988 and was extremely well developed. Thus there were only small changes this year, most of these centring around comfort and practicality. Company research told them that Gold Wing riders wanted a lower seat height, and this is what Honda gave them for 1995. Cutting 30mm from the seat height was achieved by carving 12mm off the foam and reshaping the seat. The side panels were reconfigured to match the new seat. A further reduction in ride height came through changes in the suspension. Here there was a change in emphasis from the earlier plush suspension that provided light springing without a lot of damping, to the use of heavier springs and more bump control. The result of these suspension modifications was a noticeable increase in suspension control, providing more agility while retaining the earlier comfort level. Along with the lower seat came a lower, reshaped, windshield. Given the status of the Gold Wing in Honda's line-up it was surprising that the original linked braking system continued. The ST 1100 sports tourer already featured an ABS braking system, and from 1993 the CBR 1000 had more sophisticated 'smart' linked brakes. Obviously, Honda's approach was not to mess with a proven formula, and it was difficult to

argue with this given the continuing success of the GL 1500.

The SE and Aspencade for 1995 received upgraded trunks and saddlebag liners with leather-reinforced corners and leather carrying handles, along with more front fairing garnish and chrome trunk trim. What set all three Gold Wings apart for 1995 were the distinctive 20th anniversary badges on the fairing, trunk lid and ignition key. Also included was a plaque with the machine's serial number. New colours also distinguished the anniversary Gold Wings. The SE was still available in four colour options, the new colours being Pearl Royal Magenta with purple, and Pearl Sierra Green with Toscana Green. The usual white and red continued as before except for a two-tone Italian Red with the Spectra Red. The three Aspencade colours were the same as for the SE (without the white), and were single colours only. Apart from Pearl Sierra Green joining the red, there were no other changes to the Interstate.

In 1995, this was still the most comprehensive motorcycle cockpit. Everything was easily seen or reached and the quality of the controls impeccable. (*Cycle World*)

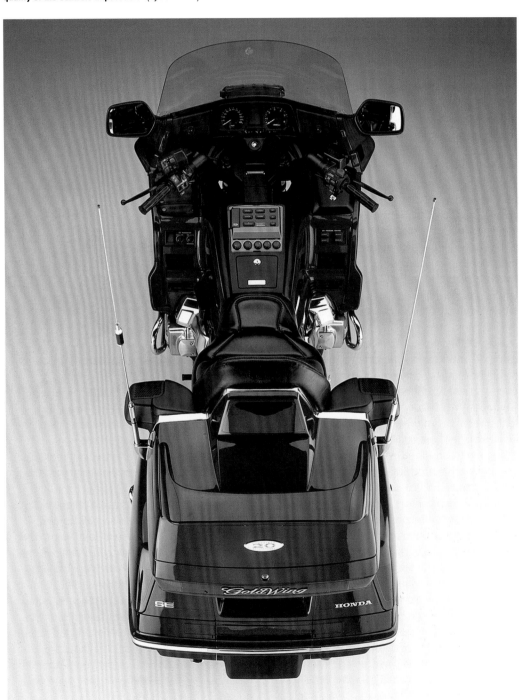

New for the 1998 SE were chrome-plated front brake covers with extra cooling vents, and yet another reshaped seat.
(*Australian Motorcycle News*)

The Gold Wing may have been 20 years old but it continued to be amazingly popular. Despite being one of the most expensive machines on the market, sales of the three versions of the Gold Wing saw it the second best-selling motorcycle in the USA during 1995. The Gold Wing was Honda's best seller, and was only beaten by the much cheaper Harley-Davidson XLH883 Sportster. Given this success it wasn't surprising that the Gold Wing continued for 1996, basically unchanged. Even the colours were the same this year, although the Aspencade now came in additional Pearl Sparkling Blue, and the Pearl Glacier White SE was two-tone, with Summer Blond Metallic. The only other improvement was the upgrading of the Aspencade audio system to a full-logic type offering easier operation. This was also the final year for the 'stripper' Interstate, the Interstate production line at Marysville now being devoted to the new Valkyrie mega-cruiser.

Further refinement of the Gold Wing was evident for 1997 when many of the upgraded engine and transmission components of the Valkyrie made it to the Gold Wing. This included higher-quality crankshaft main bearings, pistons, rings, valve springs, con-rod bolts, and final drive gear. The Valkyrie-inspired five-speed gearbox provided smoother and more precise shifting, and the clutch was strengthened. Also new were the handlebar switches which now incorporated internationally approved symbols rather than words. There were four colour options for the SE, all being slightly different to the previous model. Apart from Pearl Sapphire Black these were all two-tone: Candy Spectra Red with Spectra Red; Pearl Sonoma Green with Dark Green and Pearl Glacier White with silver. The Aspencade came in the three base SE colours (not black), but not two-tone like the SE.

Although it still looked like the Gold Wing was untouchable as the 'Best full-dress tourer' (*Motorcyclist* magazine perpetually dubbed it the

There were also redesigned cylinder head covers that featured an integrally cast '1500' emblem, along with engine guards designed to show them off. (*Australian Motorcycle News*)

winner in this category), there were a number of cosmetic changes to the GL 1500 for 1998. Both the SE and Aspencade received reshaped rider and passenger seats for improved support and comfort. There were also redesigned front brake covers that provided additional brake cooling slots. Another obvious alteration was to the fairing air ducts that now featured three-piece ABS louvres. Other cosmetic changes extended to redesigned cylinder head covers that featured an integrally cast '1500' emblem, these being accompanied by new chrome engine guards designed to show the covers to best effect. The 1998 Gold Wing was also distinguished by a white-faced speedometer and tachometer with black characters, and a redesigned headlight and turn signal lenses. The SE now featured a CB radio and came in an impressive five colour options. Black-Z made a return, and the usual Spectra Red was mated with Garnet Red. Other colour combinations were Pearl Glacier White/Ocean Grey Metallic; Pearl Chaparral Beige/Dark Chaparral Beige and Pearl Twilight Silver/Dark Twilight Silver. The 1998 Aspencade was offered in only two colour combinations: black and Candy Spectra Red.

After two years that incorporated many small developments, there were only subtle changes to the Gold Wing for 1999. This was Honda's 50th anniversary year, and each Gold Wing also came with a special anniversary ignition key and badge on the trunk and above the headlight. By now the list of factory options was considerable, ranging from a six-disc CD player to chrome panels. New colours for the SE for 1999 were Pearl Grey Green with Dark Grey Green, in addition to the usual Candy Red, Pearl White, Pearl Silver, and black. The Aspencade colours were unchanged. This year also saw the first genuine competition to the GL 1500 Gold Wing in over a decade, but this time it did not come from any of the Japanese manufacturers. With the release of the K1200LT, BMW produced a modern full-dress luxury tourer that in many respects made the venerable GL 1500 seem old fashioned. Earlier efforts by BMW to muscle in on the Gold Wing touring territory had been half hearted. While machines like the K1100LT were acceptable motorcycles, the fairing and luggage had a bolt-on aftermarket look about them. In terms of comfort and features there was still no comparison between the BMW and Gold Wing. However, with the K1200LT BMW's approach was almost Honda-like, and the machine was conceived as a complete package from the outset. It also benefited from more modern suspension, and features like an electrically adjustable windshield. While there was no doubt that the basic engine and running gear of the Gold Wing was still more than up to the task, the design was finally beginning to show its age. This was particularly evident in the design of the instruments and controls. However, despite many rumours of an all-new Gold Wing appearing, the SE and Aspencade continued virtually unchanged for the new millennium.

Continuing a tradition of Anniversary Editions, the year 2000 marked the 25th anniversary of the Gold Wing. In order to extend the life of the GL 1500 Honda seemed to be making every model an Anniversary Edition. Thus there were 25th Anniversary Edition badges mounted on the fairing chrome garnish, console and trunk. The

Another Anniversary Edition appeared for 1999, this time celebrating Honda's 50th anniversary. For 2000 there was yet another, to celebrate the 25th year of the Gold Wing. This is the 1999 SE. (*Cycle World*)

instrument faces were changed to a high-contrast type, now white characters on a black background, and the cylinder head covers were chrome-plated. The new colours for the 2000 SE were Pearl Coronado Blue/Dark Coronado Pearl Blue and Pearl White/Pearl Grey Green. Carried over from the preceding year were the Candy Spectra Red, with Candy Garnet Red, and Pearl Merced Green with Dark Merced Green.

By 2000 the GL 1500 had been in production for 13 years, coincidentally the same life span enjoyed by the 1000, 1100, and 1,200cc flat-fours. However, for 2001 the rumours of a replacement were finally laid to rest with the release of the new GL 1800. What cannot be forgotten though is the

absolute success of the GL 1500 over its 13-year production period. Even more so than the four-cylinder varieties the GL 1500 claimed the throne as the ultimate touring motorcycle. So superior was the GL 1500 in its intended role that it annihilated the competition and maintained its position for well over a decade with surprisingly little variation from the first version of 1988. Only a few motorcycles manage to stay at the top for more than a single year, and for the GL 1500 to do so for so long, with so few changes, is a testament to the absolute brilliance of the design and its execution. All that development work was vindicated and without doubt the GL 1500 was one of the great motorcycles of the 1990s.

The retro-look of the Valkyrie extended to the round headlight. Soon factory accessories such as a windshield also became available. (*Cycle World*)

The Valkyrie

Without doubt one of the motorcycling phenomena of the 1990s, particularly in the United States, was the ascendancy of the cruiser. A cruiser provided the required custom image for those affluent baby-boomer RUBs (Rich Urban Bikers), and they demanded a prestige product. Harley-Davidson had traditionally dominated this upper-end of the market, with the Japanese concentrating on cheaper cruisers, but that all changed in 1995. Yamaha released their mega-cruiser, the 1,294cc V-four Royal Star, and not to be outdone, Honda retaliated with the outrageous F6 (an abbreviation for flat-six) Valkyrie in 1996. The name Valkyrie comes from Nordic mythology, this being one of the maidens of the god Odin, who hovered over the field of battle choosing those to be slain. She then conducted the heroes back to Valhalla. It was a sombre story, and as a name to describe Honda's flamboyant mega-cruiser, Valkyrie seemed almost incongruous. In Europe the Valkyrie was sold as the F6C, indicating that perhaps Honda thought Europeans had a better knowledge of Nordic mythology.

The concept of a factory custom was not new to Honda. Virtually every engine configuration they had produced had seen some duty in a custom model. Some, like the V-twin Shadow, were even showcased as a custom before being adapted for other duties. From the first entry-level 185cc custom Twinstar of 1978, through a family of Nighthawks, Magnas, Rebels and Shadows, customs had long been integral to the Honda line-up. However, during the late 1980s interest in customs dwindled

until, in 1991, an in-house think tank, 'Project Phoenix', was organised to re-establish Honda's presence in the custom-bike market. After concentrating on expanding the custom range, it was almost inevitable that the Gold Wing too would receive a similar treatment.

With Honda's Anna, Ohio, plant able to produce many more GL 1500 engines than were needed for Gold Wing production, Honda R&D decided an additional platform for the GL 1500 engine and drivetrain was a good idea. A senior designer at Honda R&D at Asaka, in Japan, Makoto Kitagawa thus drew up the first plan in 1991. His idea was to create a performance cruiser with a strong Honda identity, with the Gold Wing engine the focal point. 'Harley-Davidson and Indian were very popular in America for a long time,' says Kitagawa. 'Honda came later to the US market. We didn't start making V-twins until 1983, so it's hard for us to have a very original position – an exclusive image – in the market. I wanted to design an original custom using a Honda identity. The flat-six engine is identified with Honda.' Kitagawa's first sketch showed a machine titled the Diablo (a name owned by the Italian car manufacturer Lamborghini) with early-Magna styling. It also featured a futuristic hydraulic drive system, a chin spoiler, hidden rear suspension, and a sporty, bobbed, rear mudguard. This was very much a performance cruiser, but it received a lukewarm response in the USA, the bike's primary market.

By 1992 Kitagawa's sketches moved more towards the retro look. After exploring performance customs, traditional cruisers, and

As the engine of the Valkyrie was more dominant visually than on the Gold Wing, many external engine parts were chromed or polished. (Ian Falloon)

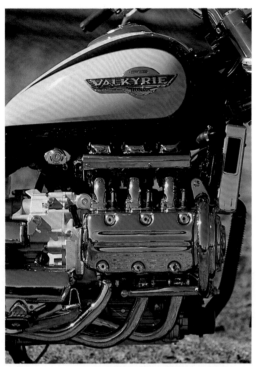

a conservative standard, the retro-style emerged as the favourite. Honda R&D North America wanted a hot-rod style, a traditional body with an uprated power plant, and the wide-mudguard Harley Heritage Softail look was very popular at that time. The fluid-drive system was replaced by a conventional shaft-drive, and dual rear shock absorbers appeared. The engine also featured six individual carburettors, something that would remain when the machine made it into production. Further sketches saw the concept move even more towards that of a retro. There were flowing mudguards, a classic teardrop-style fuel tank, and hidden front frame downtubes. After the final sketches a series of clay mock-ups was constructed during 1993 and 1994, the design team constructing two clay models reflecting different design directions. As the design needed to

complement the new-generation VT 1100 Shadow, classic styling prevailed.

In the meantime though, an early prototype was built using a modified GL chassis and engine to test the basic mechanical worthiness of the idea. From the outset the bike was considered a 'bottom-up' project, the development from Kitagawa's drawings being done by project managers and engineers further down the line rather than from managerial directives. This was known as 'blue-sky' brainstorming. Most concern centred around altering the sound of the engine. Although a high-end, high-dollar Japanese mega-cruiser category didn't yet exist, American executives wanted to extract a powerful, ear-pleasing growl from the electric-smooth and super refined Gold Wing engine. They constantly reminded the Japanese engineers of the sound and feel of American V8 engines.

The early prototypes with Gold Wing engines met with the thumbs down. They felt flat and characterless so it was decided to liven up the six-cylinder engine with more horsepower. The Gold Wing engine with its 5,500rpm redline was always tuned for mild touring performance and it was an easy operation to provide a noticeable power increase. Honda engineers employed fairly traditional hot-rodding tactics, and although the same 9.8:1 compression ratio was retained, they fitted hotter camshafts, and six Keihin 28mm diaphragm-type CV carburettors. The search for more revs saw screw and locknut valve adjusters (rather than the Gold Wing's hydraulic system), the only disadvantage now being that the valves needed servicing every 12,000 miles (19,300km). Along with a six-into-six exhaust the power climbed to 104hp at almost 6,000rpm. The maximum torque was slightly less than that of the Gold Wing, but peaked higher, at between 4,000 and 5,000rpm. The six

New for the Valkyrie were 45mm upside down forks and dual floating front discs with twin-piston calipers. (*Cycle World*)

Other factory options included leather bags and a passenger backrest. The riding position was similar to the Gold Wing and provided more comfort than most cruisers. (*Cycle World*)

separate pipes, with three enclosed in a single muffler-like casing on each side, not only provided a throatier exhaust note, they also boosted mid-range power. Everything happened 1,000rpm further up than on the Gold Wing so the electronic ignition timing was revised, with the ignition cut-out increasing from 6,300rpm to 7,300rpm. There was a new set of internal gear ratios but the overall architecture of the GL 1500 engine remained intact. What changed though was the engine aesthetics. As it was originally designed to be hidden behind the expansive Gold Wing bodywork, the automotive-like six-cylinder engine was updated visually for the Valkyrie. Many external engine parts were chromed or polished, with reshaped valve rocker covers and unsightly components such as the 546-watt alternator now hidden away beneath a chrome cover. Even the radiator trimming was chromed, and although it was a tall order to create a good looking unit out of the very automotive Gold Wing engine Honda stylists did an admirable job.

For the second prototype an all-new diamond-type frame replaced the modified Gold Wing twin-spar arrangement. Dual frame tubes went from the steering head backwards over the top of the engine to the seat/tank junction, where they curved down towards the swingarm pivot. The computer-designed heavy gauge steel tube frame may have looked old fashioned but it worked brilliantly from the onset. Testers claimed surprisingly good handling, even on the twisting Tochigi road circuit, and development was speeded up after R&D bosses rode the prototype on Alaska's Alcan Highway. They were reportedly so impressed that the frame remained unchanged. In the interest of maintaining chassis rigidity the inherently smooth flat-six engine was solidly mounted, rather than rubber mounted like the Gold Wing.

Following soon after the Valkyrie for 1997 was the Valkyrie Tourer, with a standard windshield and hard saddlebags.
(*Cycle World*)

The frame was cleverly hidden behind the 5.3-gallon fuel tank, plush seat, and plastic sidecovers, with only the steering head visible. Coupled with stout non-adjustable upside down Showa 45mm forks with massive aluminium triple clamps, and twin Showa shock absorbers, the frame displayed no hint of flex. The front forks gave 129.5mm (5.1in) of travel, while the rather harsh five-way preload shock absorbers provided 119.4mm (4.7in) of travel. In the interest of maintaining stability the rake was a conservative 32°, with 152.4mm (6in) of trail. The seat height was a low 739mm (29.1in), and as it was based on

the Gold Wing the Valkyrie was a large motorcycle. The passing of time had seen general motorcycle dimensions increase so that where once a motorcycle of the Valkyrie's proportions may have been once considered obscene, by 1996 it was acceptable. No longer was 1,000cc the optimum size for a cruiser, and the other Japanese motorcycle manufacturers had followed Harley-Davidson's lead by building cruisers displacing 1,300cc or more. Back in 1985 the Brazilian-built, Volkswagen-powered Amazonas was dismissed as a laughing stock. It weighed 384kg (846lb) and stretched a full 1,745mm (68.7in) between the axles. At 309.6kg (682lb) dry the Valkyrie wasn't quite as heavy, but it wasn't a whole lot shorter with its 1,689mm (66.5in) wheelbase.

Completing the chassis components were new cast-aluminium aero-style wheels shod with newly developed Dunlop D206 radial tyres; a 150/80R-17 on the front and a 180/70R-16 on the rear. Unlike the Gold Wing, ST 1100 sport-tourer, or CBR 1000, the triple discs brakes didn't feature any anti-lock or linked system. Twin piston Nissin calipers squeezed floating 296mm disc rotors up front, with a single piston caliper grasping a larger, 316mm, rear disc. When it came to ergonomics the Valkyrie's seating position almost duplicated that of the Gold Wing, and was quite unlike most cruisers. The ultra-wide handlebar comfortably reached back on 3in risers and there were conventional footpegs and foot controls. Rather than being a traditional cruiser the Valkyrie was more of a hot-rodded retro-machine. Because the riding position was so similar to that of the Gold Wing, long-range comfort was high, despite the basic cruising nature of the motorcycle.

Equipment included a chromed, white-faced 145mph speedometer and an 8,500rpm tachometer. Extending the retro look was a huge round halogen headlight with multi-reflector lens, and the turn signals mounted on the fork tubes in the manner of clip-on handlebars. The Valkyrie came in four colour combinations for its first year: black; black with Pearl Hot Rod Yellow; American Red with Pearl Glacier White and Pearl Majestic Purple with Pearl Glacier White.

For a large cruiser the Valkyrie set new standards of performance, and the parameters established by other large-capacity Japanese cruisers were totally obliterated. Despite a wet weight of 334kg (736lb), *Cycle World* magazine, in July 1996,

achieved a standing start quarter mile time in 12.03 seconds at 110.58mph (178kph). Top speed testing was equally impressive, the Valkyrie going through the radar gun at 128mph (206kph). Compared with the other Japanese cruisers, the Valkyrie made more horsepower, provided more cornering clearance, and weighed less than the bike on which it was based – an unusual scenario. What is more, despite the hot-rodding, the 1,520cc six-cylinder engine remained exceptionally torquey, and gear changing was virtually unnecessary once underway. Honda also claimed the Valkyrie developed greater g-forces under acceleration than their own champion sportsbike, the CBR 900RR Fireblade. More than a cruiser, the Valkyrie was a legitimate performance motorcycle, and this was evidenced by Honda's television advertising campaign in the USA. Here, a Valkyrie was pitched into an impressive dirt-track slide in a daring display of stunt riding.

It was inevitable that Honda would provide a range of accessories for the basic Valkyrie, and soon more than 50 bolt-on cosmetic and functional accessories were available. Soon after the early 1997 model year release of the Valkyrie, Honda announced the Valkyrie Tourer. The trend in big-rig tourers by this stage was also moving away from the traditional luxury full-dress Gold Wing style to incorporate a more nostalgically styled cruiser-based tourer. Not to be outdone by the impending Yamaha Royal Star Tour Deluxe, Honda too wanted a piece of this market. Ostensibly based on the standard Valkyrie, the Valkyrie Tourer came with a standard solidly mounted Lexan windshield and two colour-matched top-loading saddlebags providing 35 litres of luggage capacity. Chrome-plated metal guards bolted to the main frame's steel backbone to protect the

These accessories endowed the Valkyrie Tourer with surprisingly competent touring ability, elevating the Valkyrie beyond the other available touring cruisers. (*Cycle World*)

saddlebag's vulnerable leading edges in the event of a crash or tip-over. As tested by *Cycle World*, in May 1997, the Valkyrie Tourer came out ahead of both the Yamaha and Harley-Davidson Road King in a three-way test through Death Valley. *Cycle World* even found it superior to the standard Valkyrie and proclaimed it the 'new King of the Cruisers' because of its improved functionality. Predictably the heavier, (up to 338kg/745lb) dry, Valkyrie Tourer was a more sluggish performer than the base Valkyrie but the creature comforts provided by the windscreen in particular endowed the Tourer to the magazine's staffers. Their test machine provided a top speed of 114mph (183kph) with a standing start quarter mile in 12.69 seconds at 103.59mph (167kph). Where the Valkyrie Tourer really excelled was in top-gear roll-ons, the 60–80mph time of 4.82 seconds, rivalling many open-class sports bikes.

The Valkyrie Tourer also came in different colour options to the Valkyrie. There was no yellow or purple, there being instead a Pearl Sonoma Green with Pearl Ivory Cream along with the red and black. For 1998, the only changes to the Valkyrie Tourer were the colour options, these now being black with Pearl Jade Green and Pearl Sedona Red with Pearl Ivory Cream. As always, black remained the base colour. There were no visual changes to the regular Valkyrie for 1998 apart from colours. Along with black there was Pearl Coronado Blue, Blaze Yellow, and Pearl Sedona Red; all three with Pearl Ivory Cream. Colours for the 2000 Valkyrie were black, and black with either yellow or red. The Valkyrie Tourer was available only in black or black with red. For 2001, the Valkyrie Tourer was deleted from the line-up, but the regular Valkyrie remained. This was either black, or black with Metallic Silver, with the option of Pearl Dark Blue with Pearl White.

Sidecars and trailers

Although the Gold Wing's specification proved it to be the ideal touring motorcycle, it soon became evident that it was also provided with all the requirements for both sidecar and trailer attachment. The engine provided ample power and torque, and this was combined with a shaft drive that could handle the extra load, and a frame strong enough to accept the additional stress without complaint. Sidecars have always enjoyed a small, but fiercely loyal following therefore it was no surprise to see that almost immediately after the Gold Wing became available in 1975 the aftermarket sidecar industry made such kits available. These ranged from a simple bolt-on affair to one where Earles-type or leading-link forks replaced the stock telescopics, along with smaller diameter wheels with car tyres.

General sidecar attachment was at four points; at the front of the engine, beneath the dummy fuel tank, on the frame under the seat, and at the base of the side panel. Sidecar fitting was also more than a simple bolt-on procedure. Outfits needed to be set-up with the correct toe-in and the sidecar with

sufficient lean-out. While the standard front forks were generally adequate, a steering damper was recommended, and wider handlebars to compensate for the heavier steering. The forks also benefited from stiffer springs and heavier weight oil. Though expensive, undoubtedly the best solution for a sidecar was to replace the standard front forks with an aftermarket leading-link type, along with shorter suspension units and a smaller diameter (15-inch) front wheel.

The only problem that arose on earlier Gold Wings regarding sidecar attachment was that in the UK, with the chair on the left, the clutch cable was fouled. This was later revised. Right-side mounting often obscured the oil level sight glass but an accessory dipstick solved that problem. While adding a sidecar generally lost the motorcycle feeling of leaning through corners (unless it was an Equalean type), a trailer provided that extra carrying capacity as well as retaining all the traditional motorcycle characteristics. With Gold Wing owners exhibiting a tendency to carry a serious amount of gear, trailers have become

The Gold Wing has always been suited to sidecar attachment, as evident on this 1979 GL 1000. A fork brace is fitted in an effort to strengthen the rather flimsy front forks. (Roy Kidney)

A sidecar can look almost factory fitted as this does on a GL 1200 Aspencade. The steering damper is essential to prevent the forks juddering. (Roy Kidney)

The perfect appendage for an SE is a luxury fitted-out trailer, complete with air suspension. (Roy Kidney)

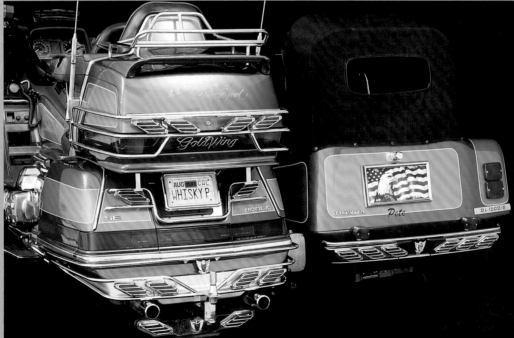

The sidecar on this GL 1500 SE has been integrated as part of the entire custom concept. If it rains Emel can stay nice and dry. (Roy Kidney)

a popular accessory, particularly in the USA where size and gadgets dominate. These have become remarkably sophisticated, being available colour-matched with lights, independent suspension, lid-mounted garment bags and even tongue-mounted coolers. The trailer hitch easily attaches to the protective and supportive tubing underneath the saddlebags. Because of the size and power of the Gold Wing, riding with a trailer is almost like riding solo, unless heavy braking or cornering is required. Here the trailer can work against the hitch, resisting the bike's lean. But for straight Interstate touring a trailer is almost forgotten, and the convenience of the additional luggage capacity difficult to ignore.

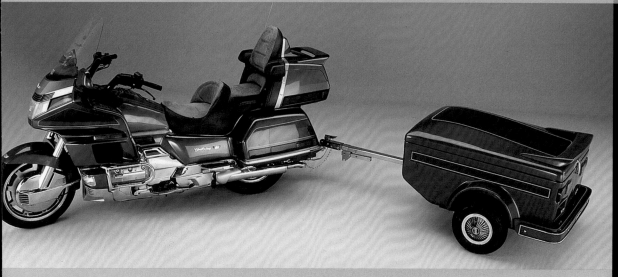

Behind this 1992 SE is a Motorvation Wingliner trailer with 20 cubic feet of carrying capacity. (*Cycle World*)

The Valkyrie Interstate

With the development of the GL 1800 well underway the top-of-the-range GL 1500 Gold Wing languished in terms of continuous development. Therefore, in order to provide new models, Honda was hard at work expanding the thriving Valkyrie line-up. From the Valkyrie Tourer emerged the Valkyrie Interstate, directly targeted at Harley-Davidson's successful FL touring series, but also designed to counteract the new neo-classic Yamaha Venture. It was almost as if the original Gold Wing had turned full circle and become reincarnated as the Valkyrie. Both the GL 1000 and Valkyrie started their life in basic

unfaired form and within a few years were transformed into the Interstate, with a factory fitted fairing and luggage.

Unlike the Valkyrie Tourer, there was more to the Interstate than simply bolting on a fairing and saddlebags. Blending retro with techno, the basic six-cylinder engine and five-speed transmission remained as before, although the ignition timing and jetting of the six carburettors was altered to improve mid-range performance. Incorporating rubber rear engine mounts like the GL 1500 increased the already impressive smoothness. The radiator sidecover routed engine heat away from the rider, and further changes in equipment included a fork-mounted fairing, larger 26-litre fuel tank, plusher saddle, full-size trunk, and a standard AM/FM radio with fairing-mounted speakers and intercom plumbing. A CB radio was optional, as were passenger speakers, but lacking though was a cruise control and cassette player.

The 1999 Valkyrie Interstate was endowed with a magnificent engine and a stable chassis, although as a tourer it was less integrated than the Gold Wing. (*Cycle World*)

As the weight increased to 350kg (771lb) dry, the frame was strengthened and the suspension firmed-up. The fairing featured a near-vertical non-adjustable windscreen, with a laminar-flow duct to minimise low-pressure turbulence. Further retro styling cues extended to the twin 40/45-watt halogen headlights encased in a chrome-trimmed multi-reflector-type lens. The riding position too was altered for the Valkyrie Interstate. A slightly narrower handlebar was complemented by an even lower 729mm (28.7in) seat height and folding footpegs. The new seat was a one-piece design, being firmer and more touring orientated. Along with the top-loading 35-litre saddlebags there was a huge blow-moulded 49-litre trunk that included a full-size passenger backrest. Also incorporated in the trunk was a row of four round taillights, just like something from an American car of the 1950s.

Colours for 1999 were two-tone black/red and Pearl Dark Green/Metallic Grey, and the Valkyrie Interstate maintained the performance image established by its other siblings. *Cycle World*, in June 1999, found the Valkyrie Interstate significantly faster and more powerful than the competitive Harley-Davidson FLHTCUI Ultra Classic Electra Glide and Yamaha Venture. Even though it weighed a considerable 371kg (818lb) wet, the Interstate powered through the standing start quarter mile in 12.45 seconds at 103.27mph (166kph). The measured top speed was 115mph (185kph). For many riders, the Valkyrie Interstate provided a realistic alternative to the heavier, and less powerful Gold Wing. It was even less 'automotive' and more 'motorcycle' with the engine on display and the array of chrome appendages. There were few changes over the next few years apart from colours. For

With a series of round taillights the Valkyrie Interstate emulated an earlier era. The low screen also led to head buffeting. (*Cycle World*)

2000, the colours for the Valkyrie Interstate were black, black with red, and Pearl Blue with Pearl Silver. With the release of the new GL 1800 for 2001 the Valkyrie and Valkyrie Interstate remained the only motorcycles with the long-serving 1,520cc flat-six engine. Colours for the 2001 Valkyrie Interstate were black with Pearl Dark Red, black with Pearl Beige, and black. With the release of the GL 1800 for 2001 it was inevitable that the larger engine would also eventually appear in the Valkyrie and a hot-rodded version of that larger unit will be eagerly awaited by those seeking the ultimate big-bore cruiser.

GL 1800 Large Project Leader Masanori Aoki with his creation. Although Aoki came from a sportsbike background he immersed himself in American Gold Wing culture in order to understand the requirements for a GL 1500 replacement. (American Honda)

The new Gold Wing

Just as the GL 1500 of 1988 was Honda's response to increased competition in their valued full-dress touring segment, for the 2001 Model Year Honda released their BMW K1200LT-beater, the GL 1800. While the appearance of the radical X-Wing prototype at the Tokyo Show towards the end of 1999 had many pundits wondering if the new Gold Wing would embrace radical suspension technology and electronic wizardry, including a navigation system, the final layout of the GL 1800 was more conservative. Despite rumours of a V-six or flat-eight, it really was no surprise to see Honda choosing to remain with the traditional flat-six engine layout and conventional suspension. After all, there really was no reason to gamble with the legions of loyal supporters. The increase in capacity provided a significant boost to torque, if not outright horsepower, and telescopic forks and Pro-Link rear suspension were already well proven. Released in Europe at the Munich Show in September 2000 only a day after its US Las Vegas introduction, the new GL 1800 created almost as much of a sensation as the original GL 1000 had back in 1974. Again it extended the parameters for a touring motorcycle, the increase in capacity making it the largest series production motorcycle in the world. This was to be Honda's most important new model for 2001, and pivotal to their goal in achieving its

One of the first concept sketches of 1996. At this stage there was still a strong association with the GL 1500. (American Honda)

three-year plan of market dominance in each segment of the motorcycle market.

Although it was still a formidable design, in many respects the GL 1500 was beginning to show its age. Few designs can weather 13 years of intense competition and the Gold Wing was no different. However, creating an all-new motorcycle from the ground up takes time, so as far back as 1993 the groundwork for development of the new Gold Wing began. Just as the earlier GL 1500 had been redesigned from scratch, so it was with the GL 1800. Thus, rather than merely update the existing design with new bodywork and a bigger engine, Honda's engineers elected to incorporate features that would not only elevate the Gold Wing to a new level, but also ensure it remained

at the technological summit in the future. By incorporating state-of-the-art equipment the GL 1800 would set new standards in safety and environmental friendliness, not only for touring motorcycles, but for motorcycles in general. In the process Honda patented 20 new technologies for the new Gold Wing. Also, responding to the general perception that the GL 1500 was more automotive than motorcycle, the GL 1800 reiterated its motorcycle emphasis. With the new Gold Wing Honda was looking at not only counteracting the BMW K1200LT, but also expanding the Gold Wing's appeal to include younger riders.

For this important project, 39-year-old Large Project Leader Masanori Aoki was brought in to head the design. This was significant because

As the design process proceeded the chosen sketches featured less bodywork to expose the engine and frame. (American Honda)

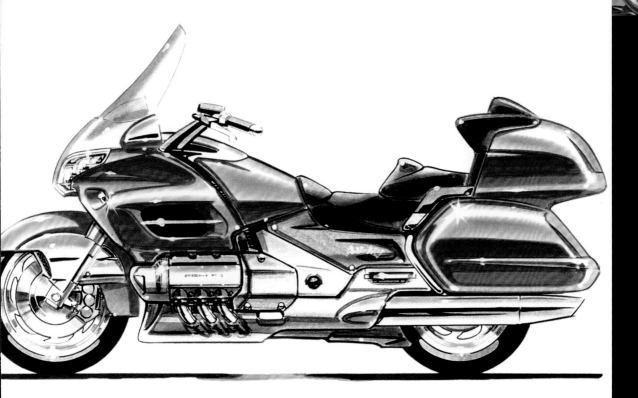

Aoki came from a more sporting motorcycle background, with motorcycles such as the two-stroke NSR250 repli-racer, and the full sports CBR250RR and CBR400R along with the CBR 600 F3, to his name. Thus it was no surprise to see a change in emphasis in the ethos of the concept. Aoki spent three years in the USA from 1993 learning English and studying the Gold Wing culture. He rode from Alaska to Seattle and attended multitudes of Gold Wing rallies. From this he learnt that the engine needed to be more powerful, especially at higher rpm, and be more fuel efficient. It needed a more motorcycle character and the touring range of the Gold Wing increased so that a touring rider could venture into more remote areas. During 1994 Honda canvassed

abroad cross-section of interested groups to ascertain the direction they should take and found that customers wanted more performance and agility. Further surveys in late 1995 and early 1996 with 23,000 owners confirmed the direction that development would take.

On 1 February 1996, Aoki returned to Japan, and on 3 February the project began. However, within the collective decision making embedded in Honda's corporate structure there was considerable lack of agreement over the design in those early days. The question centred around whether to play it safe with an evolutionary design, or try a more revolutionary approach that incorporated a decade of technological advances. The outcome resulted

Following the completion of the 1/8-scale clay models in February 1998 came the final sketch, this being achieved through a series of 3-D drawings. (American Honda)

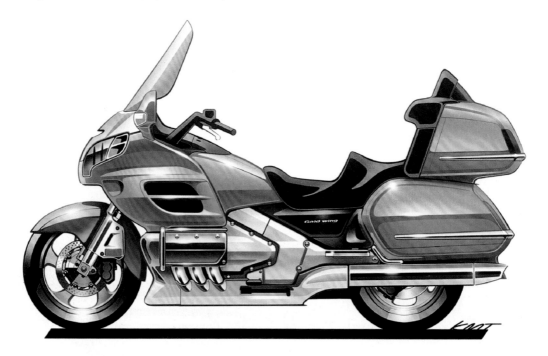

in a design that would be both evolutionary, but more importantly, revolutionary. In February 1997, Aoki and his team engaged in the first of four summit meetings to determine crucial dimensions such as the wheelbase and riding position.

By this stage, design teams from both Japan and the USA created a series of initial sketches, these concept drawings varying wildly between designers. Eventually there emerged a development theme emphasising revolution. Six design elements, sub-titled *Athletic*, were identified: Prestige (to uphold the Gold Wing tradition), Comfort, Functional, High-Tech High-Touch, Individual, and Personalisation. After these concept sketches the development moved into design images. Hundreds of sketches were eventually sorted into three design sets: Mechanical, Conservative and Integrate. The Mechanical design sketches featured less bodywork, exposing the engine

and frame, while the Conservative design sketches followed the style of the GL 1500. The Integrated look was a more flowing shape that covered the frame and mechanical components. The final decision came down in favour of two drawings from the Mechanical design set, with a competition between the two sub groups organised to determine the best qualities of each. With one sketch agreed on by October 1997, one month later groups from Honda R&D Asaka and Honda Research America set about building a 1/8-scale clay model.

Four months after the start of this modelling project in February 1998, the two models were brought together for evaluation, with an internal design team selecting the best aspects of both the American and Japanese designs. This saw some of the frame exposed and they moved on to the creation of 3-D sketches, these being necessary in order to begin both pre-

The final clay mock-up was finished in early 1999, a little over a year after the beginning of the model process.
(American Honda)

development testing and the development of specific parts and assemblies. Not only the bodywork was subjected to 3-D sketching, but also the fairing cockpit and the layout of the controls. Three-dimensional sketches of components such as the wheels and engine facilitated CAD (computer aided design) analysis and the creation of mock-ups. Knowing the importance of accessories to the Gold Wing culture, throughout the design development process there was synchronisation with the accessory development effort.

Several months after the various 3-D sketches, clay models of components were

Cutaway drawing of the 1,832cc flat-six engine. The chain-driven single overhead camshaft operated two parallel valves per cylinder. (American Honda)

completed, and with the final design approved, construction of a full-size clay model could begin. Although an extremely time-consuming process, clay modelling is more generally associated with automotive design and allows designers to carefully detail the finer exterior and interior details. In terms of production this improves the overall fit and finish as well as simplifying manufacturing processes. After consultation between the management and design team, the go-ahead was given to proceed with the final full-size clay mock-up model. A few months later this was completed, and in just over a year after the beginning of the design process, two 1/8-scale models, a full-size clay model, and a final clay mock-up had been completed.

While the general styling and overall design was progressing, Aoki's team was considering engine options for the new Gold Wing. Although a flat-four, flat-six, and even a flat-eight were considered, 'almost 100 per cent of the people we asked preferred the flat-six', says Aoki. The only question remained as to how big the new engine should be. Thus, during 1997, testing began with a heavily modified GL 1500 with a 1,657cc version of the existing flat-six. It was important to provide the optimum displacement to best meet emissions standards, and have good fuel consumption, as well as finding a balance between power, torque and weight. Testing of flat-sixes in displacements up to 2,000cc resulted in the 1,800cc version being favoured.

As Aoki says, 'ultimately it was very difficult to decide on the optimal engine displacement, so we asked American riders what size they preferred; 90 per cent liked the 1800.' Evaluation of the 1,832cc design began in April 1999 where it was tested on California's 1-15 to Las Vegas with two-up and fully loaded. The goal was to have enough power to accelerate up the Victorville Grade, and having achieved this the eventual engine size was determined as being 1,832cc.

Design parameters called for an all-new 74 x 71mm liquid-cooled, horizontally opposed 'pancake' six-cylinder engine. As the motorcycle was to be lighter than its predecessor, as well as providing more passenger and rider room, the engine needed to be more compact. It also needed to be lighter and cleaner to meet future emission controls. Thus the all-alloy engine was lighter than the GL 1500 by 1.1kg (2.5lb), and featured a completely new cylinder head design with two parallel valves per cylinder. This allowed engineers to slice off the bottom rear corner of each cylinder head, creating more room for the rider's feet.

With the entire automotive and motorcycle industry heading down the double overhead camshaft four-valves per cylinder route the new Gold Wing cylinder head design seemed almost an anachronism. However, Honda's research showed them that Gold Wing owners were not techno-heads. Gold Wing owners wanted to ride their motorcycles and not work on them, and outright horsepower was of less importance than on-the-road performance. Thus the GL 1800 retained a single overhead camshaft on each bank of cylinders, and two valves per cylinder. These were now parallel with all the valves positioned directly under the camshaft. It may have seemed that the direct, shim-under-bucket, valve actuation system was a retrograde step as far as servicing was

concerned, but valve clearance adjustment intervals were only every 32,000 miles (51,500km). The valve covers now featured 'HONDA 1800' emblems. Also changed was the camshaft drive, the earlier engine's rubber belt making way for a thinner silent-type cam chain with automatic tensioner. Along with improved rider's foot space, the new cylinder head design allowed the seat to be moved further forward. The result was that the GL 1800 rode on a slightly shorter wheelbase (1,692mm/66.6in) than the GL 1500.

Inside the engine, attention was paid to further reduce what was already an exceptionally quiet unit. As Aoki wanted the exhaust note to be appealing while retaining socially acceptable overall noise levels which meant reducing the engine noise in three areas: the crankshaft, alternator and transmission. The forged crankshaft featured high-pressure formed, sintered iron Nickalloy crankshaft bearing caps, ensuring quieter operation, and to reduce complexity and weight the water pump was mounted behind the engine and driven directly from the crankshaft. This also contributed to a quicker engine warm-up. The five-speed transmission, with overdrive fifth gear, was much as before, as was the hydraulically actuated eight-plate clutch, but the transmission featured quieter, recontoured teeth. The alternator was now a massive 1,100-watts with a dual damper system to reduce noise and minimise vibration under acceleration. Another area of improvement was in the reverse gear system. This was all-new and no longer required engaging through a separate lever. Now the simple push of two thumb controls on the right handlebar engaged the slow-speed electric reverse system. The stainless steel six-into-two exhaust system was huge, and incorporated a closed-loop emission control system.

Also revised was the cooling system, now

Two throttle bodies sat on top of the engine feeding air through long intake manifolds. Each cylinder had its individual fuel injector, positioned close to the inlet valve. (American Honda)

featuring two side-mounted radiators to assist with the positioning of the engine further forward. Similar in design to those on the VFR800FI, VTR1000F, and RVT1000R (RC51), these used low-air-pressure areas created by side cowlings to draw cooling air through the radiators and around the rider on the highway. At lower speeds (below 25kph) two thermostatically controlled fans directed cooling air through the radiators and into the fairing, away from the rider. The internal coolant flow pattern was also changed to provide a more rapid engine warm-up and to improve cold-start riding.

Although the GL 1500 had an impressively complicated multi-computer controlled induction system that worked satisfactorily, there was no doubt this intricate system was showing its age by 2000. Given the advances in electronic engine management systems since 1988, it was inevitable that electronic fuel injection would grace the GL 1800, replacing the two diaphragm-type 36mm CV carburettors. Also combining ignition advance, the PGM-F1 electronic injection system was pre-programmed and featured two digital 3-D fuel injection maps, and one digital 3-D ignition map for each cylinder. Mid-range performance was enhanced through knock control sensors which modulated ignition advance.

Grand Prix and sportsbike influence was evident in the strong twin-spar aluminium frame of the GL 1800. (American Honda)

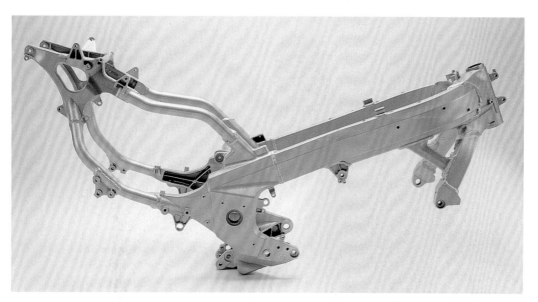

The injection system itself consisted of two 40mm throttle bodies delivering air via a large, 6.9-litre, airbox. There were six individual Keihin fuel injectors, with four nozzle tips per injector, and the system operated at a high pressure of 50psi. As before the fuel tank was positioned below the seat, this being slightly larger at 25 litres, and incorporating a PGM-F1 fuel pump. Included in the electronic injection system was a sophisticated HECS3 emission control system. This also used a central processing unit, along with an oxygen sensor in each exhaust pipe, to monitor and deliver an accurate air/fuel mixture. Twin exhaust catalysts further reduced emissions. Thus the GL 1800 Gold Wing was reputedly one of the most environmentally friendly large capacity motorcycles available with carbon monoxide (CO), hydrocarbons (HC), and nitrogen oxides (NOx) well below current and proposed European standards. It also met the California Air Resources Board (CARB) 2008 emissions standards. A rotary air control valve (RACV) provided an auto-choke function, also helping to maintain reliable idling under a wide variety of conditions. As the engine was to be a stressed chassis member it was solidly mounted in the frame, and positioned lower and more forward (around half an inch) to further enhance road holding and low-speed manoeuvrability. Without rubber engine mounts even more attention was paid to optimising balance factors and reducing high-load harmonic vibration. Featuring an identical 9.8:1 compression ratio as before, the new engine didn't produce overwhelming horsepower for an 1,800 cc unit (118hp at 5,500rpm), but was the new torque-king with 17kg/m (125ft/lb) of torque at only 4,000rpm. All along Aoki's aim was to add more character to the engine than the GL 1500 which felt like an electric motor and ran out of power too early in the rev range. As a sportsbike designer he wanted to add that burst of excitement and a more free-revving character. He also achieved his target range of more than 234 miles (376km) on a tank of fuel.

It wasn't only the engine that came in for serious development. After 13 years the chassis was beginning to look outdated as there had been significant advances both in

The new aluminium frame provided the GL 1800 with more sporting handling than the GL 1500. (American Honda)

frame and suspension design since 1988. For many years now on road racers, motocrossers, and sportsbikes, Honda had been using aluminium frames and there were now considerable technological resources at the disposal of Aoki's team regarding aluminium

frame design. The GL 1800 benefited from these developments with the steel frame of the GL 1500 becoming aluminium, and the engine being utilised as a stressed member through solid frame mounts.

The chassis requirements were for the

functions into a single component.' The result was, that while the frame was a very complex structure, it was 119 per cent improved in lateral rigidity, with 77 per cent more torsional rigidity, than its steel predecessor. The manufacturing advantages of aluminium over steel were evident as the dual-spar alloy frame used only 31 separate components as opposed to the GL 1500's steel frame and its 130 pieces. Consisting of a gravity die-cast steering head, swingarm pivots and rear suspension cross-members, these were connected by two multi-box-section extruded main spars.

Weighing 11kg (25lb) less than the earlier steel design, this box-section dual spar frame also featured specially designed engine hangers with matched mounting bolts. The finish was powder-coated silver and the design was such that the frame was engineered for an optimum balance between rigidity and flex so as to provide excellent handling along with maximum ride comfort. This concept of tuned flex incorporated in the frame design was a relatively new innovation, but Honda was a company known to place considerable emphasis on weight distribution for optimum handling. The goal was to move the rider closer to the steering head, giving a better sense of balance. Another advantage of the more forward engine location was improved ergonomics, with the riding position 50mm further forward, eliminating the previous tiller-like handlebars. In January 1998 Aoki and his development team agreed on the essential chassis dimension. 'The object was to make the steering quicker, with more direct feedback for the rider,' says Aoki. Thus the rake was set at 29.25° (compared to the GL 1500's 30°), and the trail was 109mm, 2mm less than the GL 1500. The swingarm was also shorter, with the swingarm pivot moved rearward.

One of the criticisms of the earlier Gold Wing

chassis to be as light as possible, while being stronger than before. 'These demands and limited space made the internal frame shapes very complex,' says Aoki. 'The high degree of design freedom of Honda's aluminium frame technology allowed us to build multiple

had been rear wheel accessibility and serviceability, and this was improved for the GL 1800. There was a lighter cast aluminium single-sided swingarm (Pro Arm) assembly utilising a double pipe structure. The driveshaft damping system included a rubber-bonded coating on the inner pipe to absorb engine torque and rock shocks. A redesign of the final drive ring and pinion gear assemblies saw a smaller, lighter gearcase assembly to reduce unsprung weight, now without wheel alignment splines, although still assuring accurate wheel alignment after reassembly. Now, instead of requiring professional tools, with the bike on the centrestand all that was required was the unbolting of a panel below the licence plate and removal of the wheel's five nuts. This procedure could even be undertaken with the saddlebags in place.

While there had been rumours of the possibility of an advanced new front suspension layout appearing on the GL 1800, the telescopic front forks were conventional, and not even of the upside down type as fitted to the Valkyrie. These 45mm front forks incorporated a cartridge damper in the right leg, and provided 140mm (5.5in) of travel along with a more linear damping action. Finally disappearing was the long-serving TRAC anti-dive, and the new fork now incorporated a hydraulic anti-dive system that was basically an adaptation of the system already fitted to the CBR1100XX and Interceptor. This anti-dive system included a secondary Dual-CBS master cylinder on the left fork leg, with brake fluid pressure activating the system when either the front brake lever or rear brake pedal were applied. Servo pressure from the front brake torque generated the anti-dive effect.

Rather than the GL 1500's twin rear shock absorber system, the GL 1800 now had a more usual single shock absorber mounted on a Pro-Link linkage. With more compression damping

Released in Europe at the Munich Intermot in September 2000, the styling of the GL 1800 emphasised the visual aspects of the engine and chassis. Unlike the GL 1500 the front brakes were unshrouded. (Ian Falloon)

and a more linear rebound set-up, this provided 105mm (4.1in) of travel and featured a computer-controlled adjustable hydraulic preload. This was set by push button controls and featured two memory positions. 'We developed an electric spring preload adjusting system,' says Aoki. 'A small electric motor, activated by a switch mounted on a panel above the rider's left knee, drives a hydraulic jack-type spring preload adjuster to make rear suspension adjustments easy.'

One area where the GL 1500 Gold Wing was looking outdated was in the width of the wheel rims and tyre selection. Even by 2000 the wheels were still the 3.00 x 18 and 3.50 x 16-inch of the 1988 GL 1500 and radial tyres were not fitted. While maintaining the same diameter, the sizes of the specially cast aluminium wheels for the GL 1800 went up to MT3.50 x 18 and MT5.00 x 16 inches. These also finally saw new radial touring tyres, a 130/70 R18 63H on the front and a wider and lower 180/60 R16 74H on the rear. While long-wearing characteristics were still important, radial tyres were specified to improve handling dynamics. There was also a considerably more sophisticated proportional braking system, along with an optional antilock bake system (ABS).

Although the disc rotor sizes were unchanged at 296mm on the front and 316mm on the rear, the rotors were fully floating and the rear rotor ventilated. This incorporated a steel ventilator rotor sandwiched between two twin stainless steel rotors. Unlike the GL 1500 the front disc rotors were no longer shrouded. The three Nissin brake calipers were a triple piston type, with a new dual-CBS proportional braking system that coupled all three brake calipers through a secondary master cylinder and three-stage proportional control valve (PCV). The front brake lever activated the two outer pistons of the right side front caliper, the

centre piston of the left front caliper, and the outer two pistons of the rear brake caliper. The rear brake pedal operated the centre piston of the rear brake caliper, the centre piston of the right front caliper, and the outer pistons of the left front caliper. To smooth front brake engagement from the foot pedal there was an additional delay valve sensitive to the rider's pedal pressure. There was no doubt that this proportional braking system, known by Honda as a linked braking system, provided more evenly distributed braking pressure than that of the GL 1500.

The ABS also benefited from several years of development on motorcycles in general. With an electric-motor-driven modulator this provided faster, and more accurate braking pressure adjustments. Compared with earlier systems it was also smoother and more reliable under hard braking. Incorporated in the ABS was an integrated electronic control unit (ECU) that included a self diagnostic ECU test function to protect the brakes from an ABS failure. As with the new proportional braking system this ABS contributed to the GL 1800's impressively safe braking set-up. With brake lock-up virtually impossible the ABS GL 1800 had surely the safest braking system of any motorcycle available in 2001.

Although it had stood the test of time amazingly well, the GL 1500 styling too was beginning to age. Thus, while retaining a family resemblance, the GL 1800 bodywork was all-new, with a drag coefficient 10 per cent less than its predecessor, and it was more sober and restrained. The overall height was reduced to 1,455mm (from 1,495mm) with the width down to 1,100mm (from 1,127mm). The dual headlights followed the styling trend of the 2000s, and comprised computer-designed reflectors with two 55-watt H7 low beam and two 55-watt H7 high beam bulbs. In high beam operation all four bulbs were operational. A dial

As the rider moved into a pocket of neutral air behind the
fairing, this could be smaller, with less frontal area. (Ian
Falloon)

The GL 1800's integrated luggage system provided more
storage than that of any other stock motorcycle. This is the
Pearl Yellow. (Ian Falloon)

switch on the left fairing panel provided a
motorised positioning system with 2.5° of
adjustment from the horizontal. There was also
a considerably improved windshield
adjustment system. In an endeavour to simplify
the ratchet system this was all manual, without
the weight and complexity of electric motors.
There were six settings, providing nearly
100mm of movement. The fairing also
incorporated the expected flow-through
ventilation system.

The general ergonomics too were quite
different on the new Gold Wing, with the further
forward riding position making the GL 1800
seem almost like a sport-touring, rather than
outright touring motorcycle. The saddle was

extremely low, with a 740mm (29.1in) seat
height, and incorporated the usual passenger
seat with integral backrest and side supports.
Because of the altered engine position the
passenger also received 50mm more room.
When it came to the important choice of
colours, Honda again turned to user surveys.
Eighteen months before the machine's
announcement mock-up colours were
evaluated in Ohio and Southern California. The
final selection was made six months later. For
Europe there were three colours available:
Pearl Canyon Red, Pearl Apollo Blue, and
black. For the USA there was also a Pearl
Yellow and the red was known as Illusion Red.
The Pearl Red was notable for its ability to

The instrument and display panel was more modern, and beautifully integrated in the fairing. This is the aluminium-look, and other finishes included wood and carbon. (Ian Falloon)

change the red base hue with an alteration in lighting angle and conditions. This was achieved through the incorporation of a ChromaFlair interference pigment.

While there was no denying that the new engine and chassis represented an improvement over the GL 1500, where the new version was decidedly superior was the quality of equipment. Operated from a smooth ergonomically designed right handlebar switch, the new cruise control system used a 16-bit CPU and motor-actuated throttle. This was claimed to be 2.5-times more sensitive to speed variation, with a 40 per cent more rapid response than the previous system.

As with the GL 1500 the luggage system was integral to the design, but now provided the largest storage capacity available on any production touring motorcycle. The 61-litre trunk

could easily swallow two full-face helmets, and offered an additional five litres of storage if the optional six CD changer wasn't installed. With 40 litres storage in each of the side panniers the result was a massive 147 litres. It wasn't only the extra capacity that set the new luggage system apart. With an emphasis on luxury and quality fittings, hydraulic dampers smoothed out the opening of the pannier lids and the trunk and pannier set featured a remote control key lock. This provided pop-open trunk operation and a remote lock/unlock feature for the trunk and panniers. Inadvertent remote locking with the trunk lid open resulted in the flashing of the emergency lights. The storage pockets located in the fairing and trunk included oil-damped doors, further smoothing out their operation, and all armrests and pocket covers featured a special soft-touch elastomer.

Set to maintain the 25-year Gold Wing success story, the GL1800 provides new levels of touring performance, along with the most luxurious touring platform ever offered on a motorcycle. (Ian Falloon)

There was no doubt that after 13 years the instrument and display panel was looking overly busy and out-of-date so this was one area where the GL 1800 was completely revamped. While retaining a central analogue speedometer, there was also an analogue tachometer, and coolant temperature and fuel level gauges. A high resolution 110 x 254dpi LCD displayed the odometer, trip meter, ambient temperature, audio modes, rear suspension setting, and trunk-open warning. There was also a range of warning lights for functions from overdrive to cruise set.

Equipment levels also reflected the GL 1800's intended luxury status. The multiplex audio system included two enclosed 25-watt speakers located on either side of the instrument panel, these claiming to provide improved bass output. Every known feature seemed to be included in the radio, from 12 UKW, six MW and six LW station presets to station auto select. There was even a radio data system for automatic Europe-wide reception of networked broadcasts on European specification machines. All the other usual functions were incorporated such as an intercom and automatic volume control. Much improved over the GL 1500 were the controls, with the audio console in the dummy tank and left side handlebar controls considerably more ergonomically designed. Lightweight two-piece aluminium handlebars were also used, to minimise steering inertia, and the brake and clutch levers were adjustable. Finally there were optional heated handgrips (with a thermostatic control), and an optional Panasonic CD player with a six-disc changer that fitted beneath a trap door in the top box. This was claimed to be skip-free and there were also two optional 25-watt rear speakers along with a passenger audio control.

Further attention to equipment level detail was evident in the anti-theft Honda 'Ignition

Security System' (HISS) that electronically matched the two programmed ignition keys with the ECU. Only one of these keys could start the engine and rideaway thefts were prevented as the system couldn't be bypassed through hot-wiring, alternative keys, or even installing another combination switch. As the GL 1800 experience was aimed at providing as easy life as possible for the owner, maintenance-free features included a 20AH YTX sealed battery. Along with other user-friendly features such as the electronic fuel injection that incorporated an automatic choke and idle, automatic camchain tensioner, and hydraulically adjustable rear suspension, the GL 1800 owner did not have to get their hands dirty at any stage.

As always there was a huge range of optional accessories available, and this was soon expanded considerably by the massive aftermarket. Apart from the audio options already mentioned, there was a taller windscreen, windscreen side air deflectors, and a range of saddlebag and trunk spoilers. There was also a range of pannier and trunk liners, nets and mats, seat and cycle covers, and trunk vanity mirrors and lights. A Gold Wing also wouldn't be complete without the inevitable range of chrome cosmetic accessories and special badges. Official accessories included chrome cowlings

mouldings, trims and rails, and even a chrome sidestand, so it would be a test of the imagination of the aftermarket industry to expand on these. Badges and accents allowed an owner to individualise the GL 1800 through a choice of three cylinder head cover emblems, and either wood, aluminium, or carbon instrument panel accents.

With so much at stake for Honda with the new generation Gold Wing it wasn't surprising that the design was undertaken over a seven-year period with one of the largest design teams in Honda's history. It was important not to alienate existing customers by changing the course of the design, but Honda also wanted to expand the appeal of the Gold Wing to a new, and younger, group of riders. It says much for Masanori Aoki and his design team that they have accomplished what they set out to do. They have managed to improve on what was already a formidable design by creating a long-distance luxury motorcycle with a sporting emphasis. None of the Gold Wing's comfort or amenities have been lost but they have imbued the GL 1800 with more 'motorcycle' character. As the fifth-generation Gold Wing (following the GL 1000, GL 1100, GL 1200, and GL 1500), the GL 1800 looks set to reaffirm the Gold Wing's position as the ultimate touring motorcycle, and maintain the strength of the Gold Wing culture.

APPENDIX

GOLD WING AND VALKYRIE SPECIFICATIONS

	GL 1000 1975–6	GL 1000 1978–9	GL 1100 1980–1 (Int)	GL 1100 1982 (Int)	GL 1100 1982 Asp	GL 1100 1983 (Int)	GL 1100 1983 Asp
No. of cylinders	Flat four	Flat four	Flat four	Flat four	Flat four	Flat four	Flat four
Bore (mm)	72	72	75	75	75	75	75
Stroke (mm)	61.4	61.4	61.4	61.4	61.4	61.4	61.4
Capacity (cc)	999	999	1085	1085	1085	1085	1085
Carburetion (Fuel Injection)	32mm CV	31mm CV	30mm CV	30mm CV	30mm CV	30mm CV	30mm CV
Primary reduction	1.708	1.708	1.708	1.708	1.708	1.708	1.708
Secondary reduction	0.825	0.825	0.973	0.973	0.973	0.897	0.897
Gear ratio: 1st	2.500	2.500	2.500	2.500	2.500	2.642	2.642
Gear ratio: 2nd	1.708	1.708	1.667	1.667	1.667	1.667	1.667
Gear ratio: 3rd	1.333	1.333	1.286	1.250	1.250	1.250	1.250
Gear ratio: 4th	1.097	1.097	1.065	1.000	1.000	1.000	1.000
Gear ratio: 5th	0.939	0.939	0.909	0.829	0.829	0.829	0.829
Final drive ratio	3.400	3.400	3.091	3.100	3.100	3.100	3.100
Front tyre	3.50 H19	3.50 H19	110/90H19	120/90H18	120/90H18	120/90H18	120/90H18
Rear tyre	4.50 H17A	4.50 H17A	130/90H17	140/90H16	140/90H16	140/90H16	140/90H16
Fuel capacity (litres)	19.	19	20	20.2	20.2	20.2	20.2
Seat height (mm)	810	810	795	790	780	780	780
Wheelbase (mm)	1,540	1,545	1,605	1,605	1,605	1,605	1,605
Dry weight (kg)	265	273	266 (305)	270 (308)	319	272 (311)	321

	GL 1200 1984 (Int)	GL 1200 1984 Asp	GL 1200 1985–87 Int	GL 1200 1985–87 Asp	GL 1200 1985 Ltd-E 1986 SE-I	GL 1500 1988–90 Std	GL 1500 1990–94 SE
No. of cylinders	Flat four	Flat four	Flat four	Flat four	Flat four	Flat six	Flat six
Bore (mm)	75.5	75.5	75.5	75.5	75.5	71	71
Stroke (mm)	66	66	66	66	66	64	64
Capacity (cc)	1182	1182	1182	1182	1182	1520	1520
Carburetion (Fuel Injection)	32mm CV	32mm CV	32mm CV	32mm CV	Fuel Injection	36mm CV	36mm CV
Primary reduction	1.708	1.708	1.708	1.708	1.708	1.592	1.592
Secondary reduction	0.897	0.897	0.973	0.973	0.973	0.971	0.971
Gear ratio: 1st	2.642	2.643	2.571	2.571	2.571	2.667	2.667
Gear ratio: 2nd	1.667	1.667	1.667	1.667	1.667	1.722	1.722
Gear ratio: 3rd	1.250	1.250	1.250	1.250	1.250	1.273	1.273
Gear ratio: 4th	1.000	1.000	1.000	1.000	1.000	0.964	0.964
Gear ratio: 5th	0.829	0.829	0.800	0.800	0.800	0.759	0.759
Final drive ratio	2.833	2.833	2.833	2.833	2.833	2.833	2.833
Front tyre	130/90H16	150/90H16	130/90H16	130/90H16	130/90H16	130/70H18	130/70H18
Rear tyre	150/90H15	150/90H15	150/90H15	150/90H15	150/90H15	160/80H16	160/80H16
Fuel capacity (litres)	22	22	22	22	22	23.8	23.8
Seat height (mm)	780	780	780	780	780	769	769
Wheelbase (mm)	1,610		1,610	1,610	1,610	1,699	1,699
Dry weight (kg)	272 (318)	328	317	330 (337)	350	360 (362)	365 (367) (369)

	GL 1500 1991–94 Int	GL 1500 1991–94 Asp	GL 1500 1995–96 Int	GL 1500 1995–00 Asp	GL 1500 1995–00 SE	Valkyrie 1997–	Valkyrie Tourer 1997–
No. of cylinders	Flat six	Flat six	Flat six	Flat six	Flat six	Flat six	Flat six
Bore (mm)	71	71	71	71	71	71	71
Stroke (mm)	64	64	64	64	64	64	64
Capacity (cc)	1520	1520	1520	1520	1520	1520	1520
Carburetion (Fuel Injection)	36mm CV	36mm CV	36mm CV	36mm CV	36mm CV	28mm CV	28mm CV
Primary reduction	1.592	1.592	1.592	1.592	1.592		
Secondary reduction	0.971	0.971	0.971	0.971	0.971		
Gear ratio: 1st	2.667	2.667	2.667	2.667	2.667		
Gear ratio: 2nd	1.722	1.722	1.722	1.722	1.722		
Gear ratio: 3rd	1.273	1.273	1.273	1.273	1.273		
Gear ratio: 4th	0.964	0.964	0.964	0.964	0.964		
Gear ratio: 5th	0.759	0.759	0.759	0.759	0.759		
Final drive ratio	2.833	2.833	2.833	2.833	2.833		
Front tyre	130/70H18	130/70H18	130/70H18	130/70H18	130/70H18	150/80R17	150/80R17
Rear tyre	160/80H16	160/80H16	160/80H16	160/80H16	160/80H16	180/70R16	180/70R16
Fuel capacity (litres)	23.8	23.8	23.8	23.8	23.8	20	20
Seat height (mm)	749	769	739	739	739	749	749
Wheelbase (mm)	1,699	1,699	1,699	1,699	1,699	1,689	1,689
Dry weight (kg)	345 (348)	363	349	364	370	309	324

	Valkyrie Int 1999–	GL 1800 2001–
No. of cylinders	Flat six	Flat six
Bore (mm)	71	74
Stroke (mm)	64	71
Capacity (cc)	1520	1832
Carburetion (Fuel Injection)	28mm CV	Fuel Injecti
Primary reduction		
Secondary reduction		
Gear ratio: 1st		
Gear ratio: 2nd		
Gear ratio: 3rd		
Gear ratio: 4th		
Gear ratio: 5th		
Final drive ratio		
Front tyre	150/80R17	130/70R1
Rear tyre	180/70R16	180/60R1
Fuel capacity (litres)	26	25
Seat height (mm)	729	740
Wheelbase (mm)	1,689	1,692
Dry weight (kg)	352	363

INDEX

Photograph captions are in Italics.